Harry Crecy Yarrow

A further contribution to the Study of the Mortuary customs

Outlook

Harry Crecy Yarrow

A further contribution to the Study of the Mortuary customs

1. Auflage | ISBN: 978-3-73261-873-6

Erscheinungsort: Paderborn, Deutschland

Erscheinungsjahr: 2018

Outlook Verlag GmbH, Paderborn.

SMITHSONIAN INSTITUTION—BUREAU OF
ETHNOLOGY

J. W. POWELL, DIRECTOR

A FURTHER CONTRIBUTION

TO THE

STUDY OF THE MORTUARY CUSTOMS

OF THE

NORTH AMERICAN INDIANS.

BY

Dr. H. C. YARROW,

ACT. ASST. SURG., U.S.A.

A FURTHER CONTRIBUTION

TO THE

STUDY OF THE MORTUARY CUSTOMS OF THE NORTH AMERICAN INDIANS

1

By H. C. Yarrow.

2

INTRODUCTORY.

In view of the fact that the present paper will doubtless reach many readers who may not, in consequence of the limited edition, have seen the preliminary volume on mortuary customs, it seems expedient to reproduce in great part the prefatory remarks which served as an introduction to that work; for the reasons then urged, for the immediate study of this subject, still exist, and as time flies on become more and more important.

The primitive manners and customs of the North American Indians are rapidly passing away under influences of civilization and other disturbing elements. In view of this fact, it becomes the duty of all interested in preserving a record of these customs to labor assiduously, while there is still time, to collect such data as may be obtainable. This seems the more important now, as within the last ten years an almost universal interest has been awakened in ethnologic research, and the desire for more knowledge in this regard is constantly increasing. A wise and liberal government, recognizing the need, has ably seconded the efforts of those engaged in such studies by liberal grants, from the public funds; nor is encouragement wanted from the hundreds of scientific societies throughout the civilized globe. The public press, too—the mouth-piece of the people—is ever on the alert to scatter broadcast such items of ethnologic information as its corps of well-trained reporters can secure. To induce further laudable inquiry, and assist all those who may be willing to engage in the good work, is the object of this further paper on the mortuary customs of North American Indians, and it is hoped that many more laborers may through it be added to the extensive and honorable list of those who have already contributed.

It would appear that the subject chosen should awaken great interest, since the peculiar methods followed by different nations and the great importance attached to burial ceremonies have formed an almost invariable part of all works relating to the different peoples of our globe; in fact, no particular portion of ethnologic research has claimed more attention. In view of these facts, it might seem almost a work of supererogation to continue a further examination of the subject, for nearly every author in writing of our Indian tribes makes some mention of burial observances; but these notices are scattered far and wide on the sea of this special literature, and many of the accounts, unless supported by corroborative evidence, may be considered as entirely unreliable. To bring together and harmonize conflicting statements, and arrange collectively what is known of the subject, has been the writer's task, and an enormous mass of information has been acquired, the method of securing which has been already described in the preceding volume and need not be repeated at this time. It has seemed undesirable at present to enter into any discussion regarding the causes which may have led to the adoption of any particular form of burial or coincident ceremonies, the object of this paper being simply to furnish illustrative examples, and request further contributions from observers; for, notwithstanding the large amount of material already at hand, much still remains to be done, and careful study is needed before any attempt at a thorough analysis of mortuary customs can be made. It is owing to these facts and from the nature of the material gathered that the paper must be considered more as a compilation than an original effort, the writer having done little else than supply the thread to bind together the accounts furnished.

It is proper to add that all the material obtained will eventually be embodied in a quarto volume, forming one of the series of Contributions to North American Ethnology prepared under the direction of Maj. J. W. Powell, Director of the Bureau of Ethnology, Smithsonian Institution, from whom, since the inception of the work, most constant encouragement and advice has been received, and to whom all American ethnologists owe a debt of gratitude which can never be repaid.

Having thus called attention to the work, the classification of the subject may be given, and examples furnished of the burial ceremonies among different tribes, calling especial attention to similar or almost analogous customs among the peoples of the Old World.

For our present purpose the following provisional arrangement of burials may be adopted, although further study may lead to some modifications.

CLASSIFICATION OF BURIAL.

1st. By INHUMATION in pits, graves, or holes in the ground, stone graves or cists, in mounds, beneath or in cabins, wigwams, houses or lodges, or in caves.

2d. By EMBALMMENT or a process of mummifying, the remains being afterwards placed in the earth, caves, mounds, boxes on scaffolds, or in charnel-houses.

3d. By DEPOSITION of remains in urns.

4th. By SURFACE BURIAL, the remains being placed in hollow trees or logs, pens, or simply covered with earth, or bark, or rocks forming cairns.

5th. By CREMATION, or partial burning, generally on the surface of the earth, occasionally beneath, the resulting bones or ashes being placed in pits in the ground, in boxes placed on scaffolds or trees, in urns, sometimes scattered.

6th. By AERIAL SEPULTURE, the bodies being left in lodges, houses, cabins, tents, deposited on scaffolds or trees, in boxes or canoes, the two latter receptacles supported on scaffolds or posts, or placed on the ground. Occasionally baskets have been used to contain the remains of children, these being hung to trees.

7th. By AQUATIC BURIAL, beneath the water, or in canoes, which were turned adrift.

These heads might, perhaps, be further subdivided, but the above seem sufficient for all practical needs.

The use of the term *burial* throughout this paper is to be understood in its literal significance, the word being derived from the Teutonic Anglo-Saxon "*birgan*," to conceal or hide away.

In giving descriptions of different burials and attendant ceremonies, it has been deemed expedient to introduce entire accounts as furnished, in order to preserve continuity of narrative, and in no case has the relator's language been changed except to correct manifest unintentional, errors of spelling.

INHUMATION.

PIT BURIAL.

The commonest mode of burial among North American Indians has been that of interment in the ground, and this has taken place in a number of different ways; the following will, however, serve as good examples of the process:

One of the simplest forms is thus noted by Schoolcraft: [1]

The Mohawks of New York made a large round hole in which the body was placed upright or upon its haunches, after which it was covered with timber, to support the earth which they lay over, and thereby kept the body from being pressed. They then raised the earth in a round hill over it. They always dressed the corpse in all its finery, and put wampum and other things into the grave with it; and the relations suffered not grass nor any wood to grow upon the grave, and frequently visited it and made lamentation.

In Jones [2] is the following interesting account from Lawson [3] of the burial customs of the Indians formerly inhabiting the Carolinas:

Among the Carolina tribes the burial of the dead was accompanied with special ceremonies, the expense and formality attendant upon the funeral according with the rank of the deceased. The corpse was first placed in a cane hurdle and deposited in an outhouse made for the purpose, where it was suffered to remain for a day and a night, guarded and mourned over by the nearest relatives with disheveled hair. Those who are to officiate at the funeral go into the town, and from the backs of the first young men they meet strip such blankets and matchcoats as they deem suitable for their purpose. In these the dead body is wrapped and then covered with two or three mats made of rushes or cane. The coffin is made of woven reeds or hollow canes tied fast at both ends. When everything is prepared for the interment, the corpse is carried from the house in which it has been lying into the orchard of peach-trees and is there deposited in another hurdle. Seated upon mats are there congregated the family and tribe of the deceased and invited guests. The medicine man, or conjurer, having enjoined silence, then pronounces a funeral oration, during which he recounts the exploits of the deceased, his valor, skill, love of country, property, and influence; alludes to the void caused by his death, and counsels those who remain to supply his place by following in his footsteps; pictures the happiness he will enjoy in the land of spirits to which he has gone, and concludes his address by an allusion to the prominent traditions of his tribe.

Let us here pause to remind the reader that this custom has prevailed throughout the civilized world up to the present day—a custom, in the opinion of many, "more honored in the breach than in the observance."

At last [says Mr. Lawson], the Corpse is brought away from that Hurdle to the Grave by four young Men, attended by the Relations, the

King, old Men, and all the Nation. When they come to the Sepulcre, which is about six foot deep and eight foot long, having at each end (that is, at the Head and Foot) a Light-Wood or Pitch-Pine Fork driven close down the sides of the Grave firmly into the Ground (these two Forks are to contain a Ridge-Pole, as you shall understand presently), before they lay the Corps into the Grave, they cover the bottom two or three time over with the Bark of Trees; then they let down the Corps (with two Belts that the *Indians* carry their Burdens withal) very leisurely upon the said Barks; then they lay over a Pole of the same Wood in the two Forks, and having a great many Pieces of Pitch-Pine Logs about two Foot and a half long, they stick them in the sides of the Grave down each End and near the Top thereof, where the other Ends lie in the Ridge-Pole, so that they are declining like the Roof of a House. These being very thick plac'd, they cover them [many times double] with Bark; then they throw the Earth thereon that came out of the Grave and beat it down very firm. By this Means the dead Body lies in a Vault, nothing touching him.

After a time the body is taken up, the bones cleaned, and deposited in an ossuary called the Quiogozon.

Figure 1, after De Bry and Lafitau, represents what the early writers called the Quiogozon, or charnel-house, and allusions will be found to it in other parts of this volume. Discrepancies in these accounts impair greatly their value, for one author says that bones were deposited, another dried bodies.

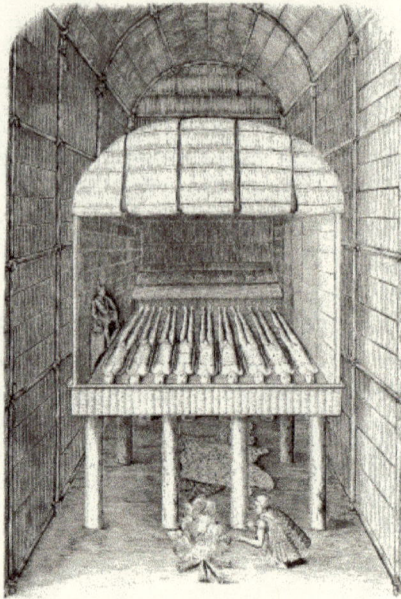

FIG. 1.—Quiogozon or Dead House.

It will be seen from the following account, furnished by M. B. Kent, relating to the Sacs and Foxes (*Oh-sak-ke-uck*) of the Nehema Agency, Nebraska, that these Indians were careful in burying their dead to prevent the earth coming in contact with the body, and this custom has been followed by a number of different tribes, as will be seen by examples given further on.

Ancient burial.—The body was buried in a grave made about 2½ feet deep, and was laid always with the head towards the east, the burial taking place as soon after death as possible. The grave was prepared by putting bark in the bottom of it before the corpse was deposited, a plank covering made and secured some distance above the body. The plank was made by splitting trees, until intercourse with the whites enabled them to obtain sawed lumber. The corpse was always enveloped in a blanket, and prepared as for a long journey in life, no coffin being used.

Modern burial.—This tribe now usually bury in coffins, rude ones constructed by themselves, still depositing the body in the grave with the head towards the east.

Ancient funeral ceremonies.—Every relative of the deceased had to throw some article in the grave, either food, clothing, or other

8

material. There was no rule stating the nature of what was to be added to the collection, simply a requirement that something must be deposited, if it were only a piece of soiled and faded calico. After the corpse was lowered into the grave some brave addressed the dead, instructing him to walk directly westward, that he would soon discover moccasin tracks, which he must follow until he came to a great river, which is the river of death; when there he would find a pole across the river, which, if he has been honest, upright, and good, will be straight, upon which he could readily cross to the other side; but if his life had been one of wickedness and sin, the pole would be very crooked, and in the attempt to cross upon it he would be precipitated into the turbulent stream and lost forever. The brave also told him if he crossed the river in safety the Great Father would receive him, take out his old brains, give him new ones, and then he would have reached the happy hunting grounds, always be happy and have eternal life. After burial a feast was always called, and a portion of the food of which each and every relative was partaking was burned to furnish subsistence to the spirit upon its journey.

Modern funeral ceremonies.—Provisions are rarely put into the grave, and no portion of what is prepared for the feast subsequent to burial is burned, although the feast is continued. All the address delivered by the brave over the corpse after being deposited in the grave is omitted. A prominent feature of all ceremonies, either funeral or religious, consists of feasting accompanied with music and dancing.

Ancient mourning observances.—The female relations allowed their hair to hang entirely unrestrained, clothed themselves in the most unpresentable attire, the latter of which the males also do. Men blacked the whole face for a period of ten days after a death in the family, while the women blacked only the cheeks; the faces of the children were blacked for three months; they were also required to fast for the same length of time, the fasting to consist of eating but one meal per day, to be made entirely of hominy, and partaken of about sunset. It was believed that this fasting would enable the child to dream of coming events and prophesy what was to happen in the future. The extent and correctness of prophetic vision depended upon how faithfully the ordeal of fasting had been observed.

Modern mourning observances.—Many of those of the past are continued, such as wearing the hair unrestrained, wearing uncouth apparel, blacking faces, and fasting of children, and they are adhered to with as much tenacity as many of the professing Christians belonging to the evangelical churches adhere to their practices, which constitute mere forms, the intrinsic value of which can very reasonably be called in question.

The Creeks and Seminoles of Florida, according to Schoolcraft, [4] made the graves of their dead as follows:

When one of the family dies, the relatives bury the corpse about four feet deep in a round hole dug directly under the cabin or rock wherever he died. The corpse is placed in the hole in a sitting posture, with a blanket wrapped about it, and the legs bent under and tied together. If a warrior, he is painted, and his pipe, ornaments, and warlike appendages are deposited with him. The grave is then covered with canes tied to a hoop round the top of the hole, then a firm layer of clay, sufficient to support the weight of a man. The relations howl loudly and mourn publicly for four days. If the deceased has been a man of eminent character, the family immediately remove from the house in which he is buried and erect a new one, with a belief that where the bones of their dead are deposited the place is always attended by goblins and chimeras dire.

Dr. W. C. Boteler, physician to the Otoe Indian Agency, Gage County, Nebraska, in a personal communication to the writer, furnishes a most interesting account of the burial ceremonies of this tribe, in which it may be seen that graves are prepared in a manner similar to those already mentioned:

The Otoe and Missouri tribes of Indians are now located in southern Gage County, Nebraska, on a reservation of 43,000 acres, unsurpassed in beauty of location, natural resources, and adaptability for prosperous agriculture. This pastoral people, though in the midst of civilization, have departed but little from the rude practice and customs of a nomadic life, and here may be seen and studied those interesting dramas as vividly and satisfactorily as upon the remote frontier.

During my residence among this people on different occasions, I have had the opportunity of witnessing the Indian burials and many quaint ceremonies pertaining thereto.

When it is found that the vital spark is wavering in an Otoe subject, the preparation of the burial costume is immediately began. The near relatives of the dying Indian surround the humble bedside, and by loud lamentations and much weeping manifest a grief which is truly commensurate with the intensity of Indian devotion and attachment.

While thus expressing before the near departed their grief at the sad separation impending, the Indian women, or friendly braves, lose no time in equipping him or her with the most ornate clothes and ornaments that are available or in immediate possession. It is thus that the departed Otoe is enrobed in death, in articles of his own selection and by arrangements of his own taste and dictated by his own tongue. It is customary for the dying Indian to dictate, ere his departure, the propriety or impropriety of the accustomed sacrifices. In some cases there is a double and in others no sacrifice at all. The Indian women then prepare to cut away their hair; it is accomplished with scissors, cutting close to the scalp at the side and behind.

The preparation of the dead for burial is conducted with great solemnity and care. Bead-work, the most ornate, expensive blankets and ribbons comprise the funeral shroud. The dead, being thus enrobed, is placed in a recumbent posture at the most conspicuous part of the lodge and viewed in rotation by the mourning relatives previously summoned by a courier, all preserving uniformity in the piercing screams which would seem to have been learned by rote.

An apparent service is then conducted. The aged men of the tribe, arranged in a circle, chant a peculiar funeral dirge around one of their number, keeping time upon a drum or some rude cooking-utensil.

At irregular intervals an aged relative will arise and dance excitedly around the central person, vociferating, and with wild gesture, tomahawk in hand, imprecate the evil spirit, which he drives to the land where the sun goes down. The evil spirit being thus effectually banished, the mourning gradually subsides, blending into succeeding scenes of feasting and refreshment. The burial feast is in every respect equal in richness to its accompanying ceremonies. All who assemble are supplied with cooked venison, hog, buffalo, or beef, regular waiters distributing alike hot cakes soaked in grease and coffee or water, as the case may be.

Frequently during this stage of the ceremony the most aged Indian present will sit in the central circle, and in a continuous and doleful tone narrate the acts of valor in the life of the departed, enjoining fortitude and bravery upon all sitting around as an essential qualification for admittance to the land where the Great Spirit reigns.

When the burial feast is well-nigh completed, it is customary for the surviving friends to present the bereaved family with useful articles of domestic needs, such as calico in bolt, flannel cloth, robes, and not unfrequently ponies or horses. After the conclusion of the ceremonies at the lodge, the body is carefully placed in a wagon and, with an escort of all friends, relatives, and acquaintances, conveyed to the grave previously prepared by some near relation or friend. When a wagon is used, the immediate relatives occupy it with the corpse, which is propped in a semi-sitting posture; before the use of wagons among the Otoes, it was necessary to bind the body of the deceased upon a horse and then convey him to his last resting place among his friends. In past days when buffalo were more available, and a tribal hunt was more frequently indulged in, it is said that those dying on the way were bound upon horses and thus frequently carried several hundred miles for interment at the burial places of their friends.

At the graveyard of the Indians the ceremony partakes of a double nature; upon the one hand it is sanguinary and cruel, and upon the other blended with the deepest grief and most heartfelt sorrow. Before the interment of the dead the chattels of the deceased are unloaded from the wagons or unpacked from the backs of ponies and carefully arranged in the vault-like tomb. The bottom, which is wider than the top (graves here being dug like an inverted funnel), is spread with straw or grass matting, woven generally by the Indian women of the tribe or some near neighbor. The sides are then carefully hung with handsome shawls or blankets, and trunks, with domestic articles, pottery, &c., of less importance, are piled around in abundance. The sacrifices are next inaugurated. A pony, first designated by the dying Indian, is led aside and strangled by men hanging to either end of a rope. Sometimes, but not always, a dog is likewise strangled, the heads of both animals being subsequently laid upon the Indian's grave. The body, which is now often placed in a plain coffin, is lowered into the grave, and if a coffin is used the friends take their parting look at the deceased before closing it at the grave. After lowering, a saddle and bridle, blankets, dishes, &c., are placed upon it, the mourning ceases, and the Indians prepare to close the grave. It should be remembered, among the Otoe and Missouri Indians dirt is not filled in upon the body, but simply rounded up from the surface upon stout logs that are accurately fitted over the opening of the grave. After the burying is completed, a distribution of the property of the deceased takes place, the near relatives receiving everything, from the merest trifle to the tent and homes, leaving the immediate family, wife and children or father out-door pensioners.

Although the same generosity is not observed towards the whites assisting in funeral rites, it is universally practiced as regards Indians, and poverty's lot is borne by the survivors with a fortitude and resignation which in them amounts to duty, and marks a higher grade of intrinsic worth than pervades whites of like advantages and conditions. We are told in the Old Testament Scriptures, "four days and four nights should the fires burn," &c. In fulfillment of this sacred injunction, we find the midnight vigil carefully kept by these Indians four days and four nights at the graves of their departed. A small fire is kindled for the purpose near the grave at sunset, where the nearest relatives convene and maintain a continuous lamentation till the morning dawn. There was an ancient tradition that at the expiration of this time the Indian arose, and mounting his spirit pony, galloped off to the happy hunting-ground beyond.

Happily, with the advancement of Christianity these superstitions have faded, and the living sacrifices are partially continued only from a belief that by parting with their most cherished and valuable goods they propitiate the Great Spirit for the sins committed during the life of the deceased. This, though at first revolting, we find was the practice of our own forefathers, offering up as burnt offerings the lamb or the ox; hence we cannot censure this people, but, from a comparison of conditions, credit them with a more strict observance of our Holy Book than pride and seductive fashions permit of us.

From a careful review of the whole of their attendant ceremonies a remarkable similarity can be marked. The arrangement of the corpse preparatory to interment, the funeral feast, the local service by the aged fathers, are all observances that have been noted among whites, extending into times that are in the memory of those still living.

The Pimas of Arizona, actuated by apparently the same motives that led the more eastern tribes to endeavor to prevent contact of earth with the corpse, adopted a plan which has been described by Capt. F. E. Grossman, [5] and the account is corroborated by M. Alphonse Pinart [6] and Bancroft. [7]

Captain Grossman's account follows:

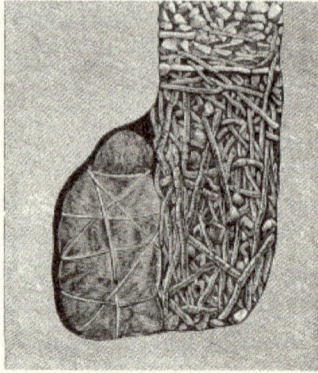

F<small>IG</small>. 2.—Pima burial.

The Pimas tie the bodies of their dead with ropes, passing the latter around their neck and under the knees, and then drawing them tight until the body is doubled up and forced into a sitting position. They dig the graves from four to five feet deep and perfectly round (about two feet in diameter), and then hollow out to one side of the bottom of this grave a sort of vault large enough to contain the body. Here the body is deposited, the grave is filled up level with the ground, and poles, trees, or pieces of timber placed upon the grave to protect the remains from coyotes.

Burials usually take place at night without much ceremony. The mourners chant during the burial, but signs of grief are rare. The bodies of their dead are buried if possible, immediately after death has taken place and the graves are generally prepared before the patients die. Sometimes sick persons (for whom the graves had already been dug) recover. In such cases the graves are left open until the persons for whom they are intended die. Open graves of this kind can be seen in several of their burial grounds. Places of burial are selected some distance from the village, and, if possible, in a grove of mesquite trees.

Immediately after the remains have been buried, the house and personal effects of the deceased are burned and his horses and cattle killed, the meat being cooked as a repast for the mourners. The nearest relatives of the deceased as a sign of their sorrow remain within their village for weeks, and sometimes months; the men cut off about six inches of their long hair, while the women cut their hair quite short.

    *   *   *

The custom of destroying all the property of the husband when he dies

14

impoverishes the widow and children and prevents increase of stock. The women of the tribe, well aware that they will be poor should their husbands die, and that then they will have to provide for their children by their own exertions, do not care to have many children, and infanticide, both before and after birth, prevails to a great extent. This is not considered a crime, and old women of the tribe practice it. A widow may marry again after a year's mourning for her first husband; but having children no man will take her for a wife and thus burden himself with her children. Widows generally cultivate a small piece of ground, and friends and relatives (men) plow the ground for them.

Fig. 2, drawn from Captain Grossman's description by my friend Dr. W. J. Hoffman, will convey a good idea of this mode of burial.

Stephen Powers [8] describes a similar mode of grave preparation among the Yuki of California:

The Yuki bury their dead in a sitting posture. They dig a hole six feet deep sometimes and at the bottom of it *"coyote"* under, making a little recess in which the corpse is deposited.

The Comanches of Indian Territory (*Nem, we, or us, people*), according to Dr. Fordyce Grinnell, of the Wichita Agency, Indian Territory, go to the opposite extreme, so far as the protection of the dead from the surrounding earth is concerned. The account as received is given entire, as much to illustrate this point as others of interest.

When a Comanche is dying, while the death-rattle may yet be faintly heard in the throat, and the natural warmth has not departed from the body, the knees are strongly bent upon the chest, and the legs flexed upon the thighs. The arms are also flexed upon each side of the chest, and the head bent forward upon the knees. A lariat, or rope, is now used to firmly bind the limbs and body in this position. A blanket is then wrapped around the body, and this again tightly corded, so that the appearance when ready for burial is that of an almost round and compact body, very unlike the composed pall of his Wichita or Caddo brother. The body is then taken and placed in a saddle upon a pony, in a sitting posture; a squaw usually riding behind, though sometimes one on either side of the horse, holds the body in position until the place of burial is reached, when the corpse is literally tumbled into the excavation selected for the purpose. The deceased is only accompanied by two or three squaws, or enough to perform the little labor bestowed upon the burial. The body is taken due west of the lodge or village of the bereaved, and usually one of the deep washes or heads of cañons in which the Comanche country abounds is selected, and the body thrown in, without special reference to position. With this are deposited the bows and arrows; these, however, are first broken. The saddle is also placed in the grave, together with many of the personal valuables of the departed. The body is then covered over with sticks and earth, and sometimes stones are placed over the whole.

Funeral ceremonies.—the best pony owned by the deceased is brought to the grave and killed, that the departed may appear well mounted and caparisoned among his fellows in the other world. Formerly, if the deceased were a chief or man of consequence and had large herds of ponies, many were killed, sometimes amounting to 200 or 300 head in number.

The Comanches illustrate the importance of providing a good pony for the convoy of the deceased to the happy-grounds by the following story, which is current among both Comanches and Wichitas:

"A few years since, an old Comanche died who had no relatives and who was quite poor. Some of the tribe concluded that almost any kind of a pony would serve to transport him to the next world. They therefore killed at his grave an old, ill-conditioned, lop-eared horse. But a few weeks after the burial of this friendless one, lo and behold he returned, riding this same old worn-out horse, weary and hungry. He first appeared at the Wichita camps, where he was well known, and asked for something to eat, but his strange appearance, with sunken eyes and hollow cheeks, filled with consternation all who saw him, and they fled from his presence. Finally one bolder than the rest placed a piece of meat on the end of a lodge-pole and extended it to him. He soon appeared at his own camp, creating, if possible, even more dismay than among the Wichitas, and this resulted in both Wichitas and Comanches leaving their villages and moving *en masse* to a place on Rush Creek, not far distant from the present site of Fort Sill.

"When the troubled spirit from the sunsetting world was questioned why he thus appeared among the inhabitants of earth, he made reply that when he came to the gates of paradise the keepers would on no account permit him to enter upon such an ill-conditioned beast as that which bore him, and thus in sadness he returned to haunt the homes of those whose stinginess and greed permitted him no better equipment. Since this no Comanche has been permitted to depart with the sun to his chambers in the west without a steed which in appearance should do honor alike to the rider and his friends."

The body is buried at the sunsetting side of the camp, that the spirit may accompany the setting sun to the world beyond. The spirit starts on its journey the following night after death has taken place; if this occur at night, the journey is not begun until the next night.

Mourning observances.—All the effects of the deceased, the tents, blankets, clothes, treasures, and whatever of value, aside from the articles which have been buried with the body, are burned, so that the family is left in poverty. This practice has extended even to the burning of wagons and harness since some of the civilized habits have been adopted. It is believed that these ascend to heaven in the smoke, and will thus be of service to the owner in the other world. Immediately upon the death of a member of the household, the relatives begin a peculiar wailing, and the immediate members of the family take off their customary apparel and clothe themselves in rags and cut themselves across the arms, breast, and other portions of the body, until sometimes a fond wife or mother faints from loss of blood. This scarification is usually accomplished with a knife, or, as in earlier days, with a flint. Hired mourners are employed at times who are in no way related to the family, but who are accomplished in the art of crying for the dead. These are invariably women. Those nearly related to the departed, cut off the long locks from the entire head, while those more distantly related, or special friends, cut the hair only from one side of the head. In case of the death of a chief, the young warriors also cut the hair, usually from the left side of the head.

After the first few days of continued grief, the mourning is conducted more especially at sunrise and sunset, as the Comanches venerate the sun; and the mourning at these seasons is kept up, if the death occurred in summer, until the leaves fall, or, if in the winter, until they reappear.

It is a matter of some interest to note that the preparation of the corpse and the grave among the Comanches is almost identical with the burial customs of some of the African tribes, and the baling of the body with ropes or cords is a wide and common usage of savage peoples. The hiring of mourners is also a practice which has been very prevalent from remotest periods of time.

GRAVE BURIAL.

The following interesting account of burial among the Pueblo Indians of San Geronimo de Taos, New Mexico, furnished by Judge Anthony Joseph, will show in a manner how civilized customs have become engrafted upon those of a more barbaric nature. It should be remembered that the Pueblo people are next to the Cherokees, Choctaws, and others in the Indian Territory, the most civilized of our tribes.

According to Judge Joseph, these people call themselves *Wee-ka-nahs*.

These are commonly known to the whites as *Piros*. The manner of burial by these Indians, both ancient and modern, as far as I can ascertain from information obtained from the most intelligent of the tribe, is that the body of the dead is and has been always buried in the ground in a horizontal position with the flat bottom of the grave. The grave is generally dug out of the ground in the usual and ordinary manner, being about 6 feet deep, 7 feet long, and about 2 feet wide. It is generally finished after receiving its occupant by being leveled with the hard ground around it, never leaving, as is customary with the whites, a mound to mark the spot. This tribe of Pueblo Indians never cremated their dead, as they do not know, even by tradition, that it was ever done or attempted. There are no utensils or implements placed in the grave, but there are a great many Indian ornaments, such as beads of all colors, sea-shells, hawk-bells, round looking-glasses, and a profusion of ribbons of all imaginable colors; then they paint the body with red vermilion and white chalk, giving it a most fantastic as well as ludicrous appearance. They also place a variety of food in the grave as a wise provision for its long journey to the happy hunting-ground beyond the clouds.

The funeral ceremonies of this tribe are very peculiar. First, after death, the body is laid out on a fancy buffalo robe spread out on the ground, then they dress the body in the best possible manner in their style of dress; if a male, they put on his beaded leggins and embroidered *saco*, and his fancy dancing-moccasins, and his large brass or shell ear-rings; if a female, they put on her best manta or dress, tied around the waist with a silk sash, put on her feet her fancy dancing-moccasins; her *rosario* around her neck, her brass or shell ear-rings in her ears, and with her tressed black hair tied up with red tape or ribbon, this completes her wardrobe for her long and happy

18

chase. When they get through dressing the body, they place about a dozen lighted candles around it, and keep them burning continually until the body is buried. As soon as the candles are lighted, the *veloris*, or wake, commences; the body lies in state for about twenty-four hours, and in that time all the friends, relatives, and neighbors of the deceased or "*difunti*" visit the wake, chant, sing, and pray for the soul of the same, and tell one another of the good deeds and traits of valor and courage manifested by the deceased during his earthly career, and at intervals in their praying, singing, &c., some near relative of the deceased will step up to the corpse and every person in the room commences to cry bitterly and express aloud words of endearment to the deceased and of condolence to the family of the same in their untimely bereavement.

At about midnight supper is announced, and every person in attendance marches out into another room and partakes of a frugal Indian meal, generally composed of wild game; Chilé Colorado or red-pepper tortillas, and guayaves, with a good supply of mush and milk, which completes the festive board of the *veloris* or wake. When the deceased is in good circumstances, the crowd in attendance is treated every little while during the wake to alcoholic refreshments. This feast and feasting is kept up until the Catholic priest arrives to perform the funeral rites.

When the priest arrives, the corpse is done up or rather baled up in a large and well-tanned buffalo robe, and tied around tight with a rope or lasso made for the purpose; then six or eight men act as pall-bearers, conducting the body to the place of burial, which is in front of their church or chapel. The priest conducts the funeral ceremonies in the ordinary and usual way of mortuary proceedings observed by the Catholic church all over the world. While the grave-diggers are filling up the grave, the friends, relatives, neighbors, and, in fact, all persons that attend the funeral, give vent to their sad feelings by making the whole pueblo howl; after the tremendous uproar subsides, they disband and leave the body to rest until Gabriel blows his trumpet. When the ceremonies are performed with all the pomp of the Catholic church, the priest receives a fair compensation for his services; otherwise he officiates for the yearly rents that all the Indians of the pueblo pay him, which amount in the sum total to about $2,000 per annum.

These Pueblo Indians are very strict in their mourning observance, which last for one year after the demise of the deceased. While in mourning for the dead, the mourners do not participate in the national festivities of the tribe, which are occasions of state with them, but they retire into a state of sublime quietude which makes more civilized people sad to observe; but when the term of mourning ceases, at the end of the year, they have high mass said for the benefit of the soul of the departed; after this they again appear upon the arena of their wild sports and continue to be gay and happy until the next mortal is called from this terrestrial sphere to the happy hunting-ground, which is their pictured celestial paradise. The above cited facts, which are the most interesting points connected with the burial customs of the Indians of the pueblo San Geronimo de Taos, are not in the least exaggerated, but are the absolute facts, which I have witnessed myself in many instances for a period of more than twenty years that I have resided but a short distant from said pueblo, and, being a close observer of their peculiar burial customs, am able to give you this true and undisguised information relative to your circular on "burial customs."

Another example of the care which is taken to prevent the earth coming in contact with the corpse may be found in the account of the burial of the Wichita Indians of Indian Territory, furnished by Dr. Fordyce Grinnell, whose name has already been mentioned in connection with the Comanche customs. The Wichitas call themselves *Kitty-ka-tats*, or those of the tattooed eyelids.

When a Wichita dies the town-crier goes up and down through the village and announces the fact. Preparations are immediately made for the burial, and the body is taken without delay to the grave prepared for its reception. If the grave is some distance from the village, the body is carried thither on the back of a pony, being first wrapped in blankets and then laid prone, across the saddle, one person walking on either side to support it. The grave is dug from three to four feet deep and of sufficient length for the extended body. First blankets and buffalo-robes are laid in the bottom of the grave, then the body, being taken from the horse and unwrapped, is dressed in its best apparel and with ornaments is placed upon a couch of blankets and robes, with the head towards the west and the feet to the east; the valuables belonging to the deceased are placed with the body in the grave. With the man are deposited his bows and arrows or gun, and with the woman her cooking utensils and other implements of her toil. Over the body sticks are placed six or eight inches deep and grass over these, so that when the earth is filled in, it need not come in contact with the body or its trappings. After the grave is filled with earth, a pen of poles is built around it, or as is frequently the case, stakes are driven so that they cross each other from either side about midway over the grave, thus forming a complete protection from the invasion of wild animals. After all this is done, the grass or other *debris* is carefully scraped from about the grave for several feet, so that the ground is left smooth and clean. It is seldom the case that the relatives accompany the remains to the grave, but they more often employ others to bury the body for them, usually women. Mourning is similar in this tribe, as in others, and it consists in cutting off the hair, fasting, &c. Horses are also killed at the grave.

The Caddoes, *Ascena*, or Timber Indians, as they call themselves, follow nearly the same mode of burial as the Wichitas, but one custom prevailing is worthy of mention:

If a Caddo is killed in battle, the body is never buried, but is left to be devoured by beasts or birds of prey, and the condition of such individuals in the other world is considered to be far better than that of persons dying a natural death.

In a work by Bruhier [9] the following remarks, freely translated by the writer, may be found, which note a custom having great similarity to the exposure of bodies to wild beasts mentioned above:

The ancient Persians threw out the bodies of their dead on the roads, and if they were promptly devoured by wild beasts it was esteemed a great honor, a misfortune if not. Sometimes they interred, always wrapping the dead in a wax cloth to prevent odor.

M. Pierre Muret, [10] from whose book Bruhier probably obtained his information, gives at considerable length an account of this peculiar method of treating the dead among the Persians, as follows:

It is a matter of astonishment, considering the *Persians* have ever had the renown of being one of the most civilized Nations in the world, that notwithstanding they should have used such barbarous customs about the Dead as are set down in the Writings of some Historians; and the rather because at this day there are still to be seen among them those remains of Antiquity, which do fully satisfie us, that their Tombs have been very magnificent. And yet nevertheless, if we will give credit to *Procopius* and *Agathias*, the *Persians* were never wont to bury their Dead Bodies, so far were they from bestowing any Funeral

Honours upon them: But, as these Authors tell us, they exposed them stark naked in the open fields, which is the greatest shame our Laws do allot to the most infamous Criminals, by laying them open to the view of all upon the highways: Yea, in their opinion it was a great unhappiness, if either Birds or Beasts did not devour their Carcases; and they commonly made an estimate of the Felicity of these poor Bodies, according as they were sooner or later made a prey of. Concerning these, they resolved that they must needs have been very bad indeed, since even the beasts themselves would not touch them; which caused an extream sorrow to their Relations, they taking it for an ill boding to their Family, and an infallible presage of some great misfortune hanging over their heads; for they persuaded themselves, that the Souls which inhabited those Bodies being dragg'd into Hell, would not fail to come and trouble them; and that being always accompanied with the Devils, their Tormentors, they would certainly give them a great deal of disturbance.

And on the contrary, when these Corpses were presently devoured, their joy was very great, they enlarged themselves in praises of the Deceased; every one esteeming them undoubtedly happy, and came to congratulate their relations on that account: For as they believed assuredly, that they were entered into the *Elysian* Fields, so they were persuaded, that they would procure the same bliss for all those of their family.

They also took a great delight to see Skeletons and Bones scatered up and down in the fields, whereas we can scarcely endure to see those of Horses and Dogs used so. And these remains of Humane Bodies, (the sight whereof gives us so much horror, that we presently bury them out of our sight, whenever we find them elsewhere than in Charnel-houses or Church-yards) were the occasion of their greatest joy; beecause they concluded from thence the happiness of those that had been devoured, wishing after their Death to meet with the like good luck.

The same author states, and Bruhier corroborates the assertion, that the Parthians, Medes, Iberians, Caspians, and a few others, had such a horror and aversion of the corruption and decomposition of the dead, and of their being eaten by worms, that they threw out the bodies into the open fields to be devoured by wild beasts, a part of their belief being that persons so devoured would not be entirely extinct, but enjoy at least a partial sort of life in their living sepulchers. It is quite probable that for these and other reasons the

Bactrians and Hircanians trained dogs for this special purpose, called *Canes sepulchrales*, which received the greatest care and attention, for it was deemed proper that the souls of the deceased should have strong and lusty frames to dwell in.

The Buddhists of Bhotan are said to expose the bodies of their dead on top of high rocks.

According to Tegg, whose work is quoted frequently, in the London Times of January 28, 1876, Mr. Monier Williams writes from Calcutta regarding the "Towers of Silence," so called, of the Parsees, who, it is well known, are the descendants of the ancient Persians expelled from Persia by the Mohammedan conquerors, and settled at Surat about 1,100 years since. This gentleman's narrative is freely made use of to show how the custom of the exposure of the dead to birds of prey has continued up to the present time.

> The Dakhmas, or Parsee towers of silence, are erected in a garden on the highest point of Malabar Hill, a beautiful, rising ground on one side of Black Bay, noted for the bungalows and compounds of the European and wealthier inhabitants of Bombay scattered in every direction over its surface.

> The garden is approached by a well-constructed, private road, all access to which, except to Parsees, is barred by strong iron gates.

The garden is described as being very beautiful, and he says:

> No English nobleman's garden could be better kept, and no pen could do justice to the glories of its flowering shrubs, cypresses, and palms. It seemed the very ideal, not only of a place of sacred silence, but of peaceful rest.

The towers are five in number, built of hardest black granite, about 40 feet in diameter and 25 in height, and constructed so solidly as almost to resist absolutely the ravages of time. The oldest and smallest of the towers was constructed about 200 years since, when the Parsees first settled in Bombay, and is used only for a certain family. The next oldest was erected in 1756, and the three others during the next century. A sixth tower of square shape stands alone, and is only used for criminals.

The writer proceeds as follows:

> Though wholly destitute of ornament and even of the simplest moldings, the parapet of each tower possesses an extraordinary coping, which instantly attracts and fascinates the gaze. It is a coping

formed not of dead stone, but of living vultures. These birds, on the occasion of my visit, had settled themselves side by side in perfect order and in a complete circle around the parapets of the towers, with their heads pointing inwards, and so lazily did they sit there, and so motionless was their whole mien, that except for their color, they might have been carved out of the stonework.

F_{IG}. 3.—Parsee Towers of Silence (interior).

No one is allowed to enter the towers except the corpse-bearers, nor is any one permitted within thirty feet of the immediate precincts. A model was shown Mr. Williams, and from it he drew up this description:

Imagine a round column or massive cylinder, 12 or 14 feet high and at least 40 feet in diameter, built throughout of solid stone except in the center, where a well, 5 or 6 feet across, leads down to an excavation under the masonry, containing four drains at right angles to each other, terminated by holes filled with charcoal. Round the upper surface of this solid circular cylinder, and completely hiding the interior from view, is a stone parapet, 10 or 12 feet in height. This it is which, when viewed from the outside, appears to form one piece with the solid stone-work, and being, like it, covered with chunam, gives the whole the appearance of a low tower. The upper surface of the solid stone column is divided into 72 compartments, or open receptacles, radiating like the spokes of a wheel from the central well, and arranged in three concentric rings, separated from each other by narrow ridges of stone, which are grooved to act as channels for conveying all moisture from the receptacles into the well and into the lower drains. It should be noted that the number "3" is emblematical of Zoroaster's three precepts, and the number "72" of the chapters of his Yasna, a portion of the Zend-Avestá.

Each circle of open stone coffins is divided from the next by a pathway, so that there are three circular pathways, the last encircling the central well, and these three pathways are crossed by another pathway conducting from the solitary door which admits the corpse-bearers from the exterior. In the outermost circle of the stone coffins are placed the bodies of males, in the middle those of the females, and in the inner and smallest circle nearest the well those of children.

While I was engaged with the secretary in examining the model, a sudden stir among the vultures made us raise our heads. At least a hundred birds collected round one of the towers began to show symptoms of excitement, while others swooped down from neighboring trees. The cause of this sudden abandonment of their previous apathy soon revealed itself. A funeral was seen to be approaching. However distant the house of a deceased person, and whether he be rich or poor, high or low in rank, his body is always carried to the towers by the official corpse-bearers, called *Nasasalár*, who form a distinct class, the mourners walking behind.

Before they remove the body from the house where the relatives are assembled, funeral prayers are recited, and the corpse is exposed to the gaze of a dog, regarded by the Parsees as a sacred animal. This latter ceremony is called *sagdid*.

Then the body, swathed in a white sheet, is placed in a curved metal trough, open at both ends, and the corpse-bearers, dressed in pure white garments, proceed with it towards the towers. They are followed by the mourners at a distance of at least 30 feet, in pairs, also dressed in white, and each couple joined by holding a white handkerchief between them. The particular funeral I witnessed was that of a child. When the two corpse-bearers reached the path leading by a steep incline to the door of the tower, the mourners, about eight in number, turned back and entered one of the prayer-houses. "There," said the secretary, "they repeat certain gáthás, and pray that the spirit of the deceased may be safely transported, on the fourth day after death, to its final resting-place."

The tower selected for the present funeral was one in which other members of the same family had before been laid. The two bearers speedily unlocked the door, reverently conveyed the body of the child into the interior, and, unseen by any one, laid it uncovered in one of the open stone receptacles nearest the central well. In two minutes they reappeared with the empty bier and white cloth, and scarcely had they closed the door when a dozen vultures swooped down upon the body and were rapidly followed by others. In five minutes more we saw the satiated birds fly back and lazily settle down again upon the parapet. They had left nothing behind but a skeleton. Meanwhile, the bearers were seen to enter a building shaped like a high barrel. There, as the secretary informed me, they changed their clothes and washed themselves. Shortly afterwards we saw them come out and deposit their cast-off funeral garments in a stone receptacle near at hand. Not a thread leaves the garden, lest it should carry defilement into the city. Perfectly new garments are supplied at each funeral. In a fortnight, or, at most, four weeks, the same bearers return, and, with gloved hands and implements resembling tongs, place the dry skeleton in the central well. There the bones find their last resting-place, and there the dust of whole generations of Parsees commingling is left undisturbed for centuries.

The revolting sight of the gorged vultures made me turn my back on the towers with ill-concealed abhorrence. I asked the secretary how it was possible to become reconciled to such usage. His reply was nearly in the following words: "Our prophet Zoroaster, who lived 6,000 years ago, taught us to regard the elements as symbols of the Deity. Earth, fire, water, he said, ought never, under any circumstances, to be defiled by contact with putrefying flesh. Naked, he said, came we into the world and naked we ought to leave it. But the decaying particles of our bodies should be dissipated as rapidly as possible and in such a way that neither Mother Earth nor the beings she supports should be

26

contaminated in the slightest degree. In fact, our prophet was the greatest of health officers, and, following his sanitary laws, we build our towers on the tops of the hills, above all human habitations. We spare no expense in constructing them of the hardest materials, and we expose our putrescent bodies in open stone receptacles, resting on fourteen feet of solid granite, not necessarily to be consumed by vultures, but to be dissipated in the speediest possible manner and without the possibility of polluting the earth or contaminating a single being dwelling thereon. God, indeed, sends the vultures, and, as a matter of fact, these birds do their appointed work much more expeditiously than millions of insects would do if we committed our bodies to the ground. In a sanitary point of view, nothing can be more perfect than our plan. Even the rain-water which washes our skeletons is conducted by channels into purifying charcoal. Here in these five towers rest the bones of all the Parsees that have lived in Bombay for the last two hundred years. We form a united body in life and we are united in death."

It would appear that the reasons given for this peculiar mode of disposing of the dead by the Parsee secretary are quite at variance with the ideas advanced by Muret regarding the ancient Persians, and to which allusion has already been made. It might be supposed that somewhat similar motives to those governing the Parsees actuated those of the North American Indians who deposit their dead on scaffolds and trees, but the theory becomes untenable when it is recollected that great care is taken to preserve the dead from the ravages of carnivorous birds, the corpse being carefully enveloped in skins and firmly tied up with ropes or thongs.

Figures 3 and 4 are representations of the Parsee towers of silence, drawn by Mr. Holmes, mainly from the description given.

F_{IG}. 4.—Parsee Towers of Silence.

George Gibbs [11] gives the following account of burial among the Klamath and Trinity Indians of the Northwest coast, the information having been originally furnished him by James G. Swan.

> The graves, which are in the immediate vicinity of their houses, exhibit very considerable taste and a laudable care. The dead are inclosed in rude coffins formed by placing four boards around the body, and covered with earth to some depth; a heavy plank, often supported by upright head and foot stones, is laid upon the top, or stones are built up into a wall about a foot above the ground, and the top flagged with others. The graves of the chiefs are surrounded by neat wooden palings, each pale ornamented with a feather from the tail of the bald eagle. Baskets are usually staked down by the side, according to the wealth or popularity of the individual, and sometimes other articles for ornament or use are suspended over them. The funeral ceremonies occupy three days, during which the soul of the deceased is in danger from *O-mah-á*, or the devil. To preserve it from this peril, a fire is kept up at the grave, and the friends of the deceased howl around it to scare away the demon. Should they not be successful in this the soul is carried down the river, subject, however, to redemption by *Péh-ho-wan* on payment of a big knife. After the expiration of three days it is all well with them.

The question may well be asked, is the big knife a "sop to Cerberus"?

To Dr. Charles E. McChesney, acting assistant surgeon, United States Army,

28

one of the most conscientious and careful of observers, the writer is indebted for the following interesting account of the mortuary customs of the

WAH-PETON AND SISSETON SIOUX OF DAKOTA.

A large proportion of these Indians being members of the Presbyterian church (the missionaries of which church have labored among them for more than forty years past), the dead of their families are buried after the customs of that church, and this influence is felt to a great extent among those Indians who are not strict church members, so that they are dropping one by one the traditional customs of their tribe, and but few can now be found who bury their dead in accordance with their customs of twenty or more years ago. The dead of those Indians who still adhere to their modern burial customs are buried in the ways indicated below.

Warrior.—After death they paint a warrior red across the mouth, or they paint a hand in black color, with the thumb on one side of the mouth and the fingers separated on the other cheek, the rest of the face being painted red. (This latter is only done as a mark of respect to a specially brave man.) Spears, clubs, and the medicine-bag of the deceased when alive are buried with the body, the medicine-bag being placed on the bare skin over the region of the heart. There is not now, nor has there been, among these Indians any special preparation of the grave. The body of a warrior is generally wrapped in a blanket or piece of cloth (and frequently in addition is placed in a box) and buried in the grave prepared for the purpose, always, as the majority of these Indians inform me, with the head towards the *south*. (I have, however, seen many graves in which the head of the occupant had been placed to the *east*. It may be that these graves were those of Indians who belonged to the church; and a few Indians inform me that the head is sometimes placed towards the *west*, according to the occupant's belief when alive as to the direction from which his guiding medicine came, and I am personally inclined to give credence to this latter as sometimes occurring.) In all burials, when the person has died a natural death, or had not been murdered, and whether man, woman, or child, the body is placed in the grave with the face *up*. In cases, however, when a man or woman has been murdered by one of their own tribe, the body was, and is always, placed in the grave with the face *down*, head to the *south*, and a piece of fat (bacon or pork) placed in the mouth. This piece of fat is placed in the mouth, as these

Indians say, to prevent the spirit of the murdered person driving or scaring the game from that section of country. Those Indians who state that their dead are always buried with the head towards the south say they do so in order that the spirit of the deceased may go to the south, the land from which these Indians believe they originally came.

Women and children.—Before death the face of the person expected to die is often painted in a red color. When this is not done before death it is done afterwards; the body being then buried in a grave prepared for its reception, and in the manner described for a warrior, cooking-utensils taking the place of the warrior's weapons. In cases of boys and girls a kettle of cooked food is sometimes placed at the head of the grave after the body is covered. Now, if the dead body be that of a boy, all the boys of about his age go up and eat of the food, and in cases of girls all the girls do likewise. This, however, has never obtained as a custom, but is sometimes done in cases of warriors and women also.

Cremation has never been practiced by these Indians. It is now, and always has been, a custom among them to remove a lock of hair from the top or scalp lock of a warrior, or from the left side of the head of a woman, which is carefully preserved by some near relative of the deceased, wrapped in pieces of calico and muslin, and hung in the lodge of the deceased and is considered the ghost of the dead person. To the bundle is attached a tin cup or other vessel, and in this is placed some food for the spirit of the dead person. Whenever a stranger happens in at meal time, this food, however, is not allowed to go to waste; if not consumed by the stranger to whom it is offered, some of the occupants of the lodge eat it. They seem to take some pains to please the ghost of the deceased, thinking thereby they will have good luck in their family so long as they continue to do so. It is a custom with the men when they smoke to offer the pipe to the ghost, at the same time asking it to confer some favor on them, or aid them in their work or in hunting, &c.

There is a feast held over this bundle containing the ghost of the deceased, given by the friends of the dead man. This feast may be at any time, and is not at any particular time, occurring, however, generally as often as once a year, unless, at the time of the first feast, the friends designate a particular time, such, for instance, as when the leaves fall, or when the grass comes again. This bundle is never permitted to leave the lodge of the friends of the dead person, except to be buried in the grave of one of them. Much of the property of the deceased person is buried with the body, a portion being placed under the body and a portion over it. Horses are sometimes killed on the grave of a warrior, but this custom is gradually ceasing, in consequence of the value of their ponies. These animals are therefore now generally given away by the person before death, or after death disposed of by the near relatives. Many years ago it was customary to kill one or more ponies at the grave. In cases of more than ordinary wealth for an Indian, much of his personal property is now, and has ever been, reserved from burial with the body, and forms the basis for a gambling party, which will be described hereafter. No food is ever buried in the grave, but some is occasionally placed at the head of it; in which case it is consumed by the friends of the dead person. Such is the method that was in vogue with these Indians twenty years ago, and which is still adhered to, with more or less exactness, by the majority of them, the exceptions being those who are strict church members and those very few families who adhere to their ancientcustoms.

Before the year 1860 it was a custom, for as long back as the oldest members of these tribes can remember, and with the usual tribal traditions handed down from generation to generation, in regard to this as well as to other things, for these Indians to bury in a tree or on a platform, and in those days an Indian was only buried in the ground as a mark of disrespect in consequence of the person having been murdered, in which case the body would be buried in the ground, *face down*, head toward the south and with a piece of fat in the mouth.
 * * * The platform upon which the body was deposited was constructed of four crotched posts firmly set in the ground, and connected near the top by cross-pieces, upon which was placed boards, when obtainable, and small sticks of wood, sometimes hewn so as to give a firm resting-place for the body. This platform had an elevation of from six to eight or more feet, and never contained but one body, although frequently having sufficient surface to accommodate two or three. In burying in the crotch of a tree and on platforms, the head of the dead person was always placed towards the south; the body was wrapped in blankets or pieces of cloth securely tied, and many of the personal effects of the deceased were buried with it; as in the case of a warrior, his bows and arrows, war-clubs, &c., would be placed alongside of the body, the Indians saying he would need such things in the next world.

I am informed by many of them that it was a habit, before their outbreak, for some to carry the body of a near relative whom they held in great respect with them on their moves, for a greater or lesser time, often as long as two or three years before burial. This, however, never obtained generally among them, and some of them seem to know nothing about it. It has of late years been entirely dropped, except when a person dies away from home, it being then customary for the friends to bring the body home for burial.

Mourning ceremonies.—The mourning ceremonies before the year 1860 were as follows: After the death of a warrior the whole camp or tribe would be assembled in a circle, and after the widow had cut herself on the arms, legs, and body with a piece of flint, and removed the hair from her head, she would go around the ring any number of times she chose, but each time was considered as an oath that she would not marry for a year, so that she could not marry for as many years as times she went around the circle. The widow would all this time keep up a crying and wailing. Upon the completion of this the friends of the deceased would take the body to the platform or tree where it was to remain, keeping up all this time their wailing and crying. After depositing the body, they would stand under it and continue exhibiting their grief, the squaws by hacking their arms and legs with flint and cutting off the hair from their head. The men would sharpen sticks and run them through the skin of their arms and legs, both men and women keeping up their crying generally for the remainder of the day, and the near relatives of the deceased for several days thereafter. As soon as able, the warrior friends of the deceased would go to a near tribe of their enemies and kill one or more of them if possible, return with their scalps, and exhibit them to the deceased person's relatives, after which their mourning ceased, their friends considering his death as properly avenged; this, however, was many years ago, when their enemies were within reasonable striking distance, such, for instance, as the Chippewas and the Arickarees, Gros Ventres and Mandan Indians. In cases of women and children, the squaws would cut off their hair, hack their persons with flint, and sharpen sticks and run them through the skin of the arms and legs, crying as for a warrior.

It was an occasional occurrence twenty or more years ago for a squaw when she lost a favorite child to commit suicide by hanging herself with a lariat over the limb of a tree. This could not have prevailed to any great extent, however, although the old men recite several instances of its occurrence, and a very few examples within recent years. Such was their custom before the Minnesota outbreak, since which time it has gradually died out, and at the present time these ancient customs are adhered to by but a single family, known as the seven brothers, who appear to retain all the ancient customs of their tribe. At the present time, as a mourning observance, the squaws hack themselves on their legs with knives, cut off their hair, and cry and wail around the grave of the dead person, and the men in addition paint their faces, but no longer torture themselves by means of sticks passed through the skin of the arms and legs. This cutting and painting is sometimes done before and sometimes after the burial of the body. I also observe that many of the women of these tribes are adopting so much of the customs of the whites as prescribes the wearing of black for certain periods. During the period of mourning these Indians never wash their face, or comb their hair, or laugh. These customs are observed with varying degree of strictness, but not in many instances with that exactness which characterized these Indians before the advent of the white man among them. There is not now any permanent mutilation of the person practiced as a mourning ceremony by them. That mutilation of a finger by removing one or more joints, so generally observed among the Minnetarree Indians at the Fort Berthold, Dak., Agency, is not here seen, although the old men of these tribes inform me that it was an ancient custom among their women, on the occasion of the burial of a husband, to cut off a portion of a finger and have it suspended in the tree above his body. I have, however, yet to see an example of this having been done by any of the Indians now living, and the custom must have fallen into disuse more than seventy years ago.

In regard to the period of mourning, I would say that there does not now appear to be, and, so far as I can learn, never was, any fixed period of mourning, but it would seem that, like some of the whites, they mourn when the subject is brought to their minds by some remark or other occurrence. It is not unusual at the present time to hear a man or woman cry and exclaim, "O, my poor husband!" "O, my poor wife!" or "O, my poor child!" as the case may be, and, upon inquiring, learn that the event happened several years before. I have elsewhere mentioned that in some cases much of the personal property of the deceased was and is reserved from burial with the body, and forms the basis of a gambling party. I shall conclude my remarks upon the burial customs, &c., of these Indians by an account of this, which they designate as the "ghost's gamble."

The account of the game will be found in another part of this paper.

As illustrative of the preparation of the dead Indian warrior for the tomb, a translation of Schiller's beautiful burial song is here given. It is believed to be by Bulwer, and for it the writer is indebted to the kindness of Mr. Benjamin Drew, of Washington, D.C.:

BURIAL OF THE CHIEFTAIN.

See on his mat, as if of yore,
    How lifelike sits he here;
With the same aspect that he wore
    When life to him was dear.
But where the right arm's strength, and where
    The breath he used to breathe
To the Great Spirit aloft in air,
    The peace-pipe's lusty wreath?
And where the hawk-like eye, alas!
    That wont the deer pursue
Along the waves of rippling grass,
    Or fields that shone with dew?
Are these the limber, bounding feet

34

That swept the winter snows?
What startled deer was half so fleet,
   Their speed outstripped the roe's.
These hands that once the sturdy bow
   Could supple from its pride,
How stark and helpless hang they now
   Adown the stiffened side!
Yet weal to him! at peace he strays
   Where never fall the snows,
Where o'er the meadow springs the maize
   That mortal never sows;
Where birds are blithe in every brake,
   Where forests teem with deer,
Where glide the fish through every lake,
   One chase from year to year!
With spirits now he feasts above;
   All left us, to revere
The deeds we cherish with our love,
   The rest we bury here.
Here bring the last gifts, loud and shrill
   Wail death-dirge of the brave
What pleased him most in life may still
   Give pleasure in the grave.
We lay the axe beneath his head
   He swung when strength was strong,
The bear on which his hunger fed—
   The way from earth is long!
And here, new-sharpened, place the knife

Which severed from the clay,

From which the axe had spoiled the life,

The conquered scalp away.

The paints that deck the dead bestow,

Aye, place them in his hand,

That red the kingly shade may glow

Amid the spirit land.

The position in which the body is placed, as mentioned by Dr. McChesney, face upwards, while of common occurrence among most tribes of Indians, is not invariable as a rule, for the writer discovered at a cemetery belonging to an ancient pueblo in the valley of the Chama, near Abiquiu, N.Mex., a number of bodies, all of which had been buried face downward. The account originally appeared in Field and Forest, 1877, vol. iii, No. 1, p. 9.

On each side of the town were noticed two small arroyas or water washed ditches, within 30 feet of the walls, and a careful examination of these revealed the objects of our search. At the bottom of the arroyas, which have certainly formed subsequent to the occupation of the village, we found portions of human remains, and following up the walls of the ditch soon had the pleasure of discovering several skeletons *in situ*. The first found was in the eastern arroya, and the grave in depth was nearly 8 feet below the surface of the mesa. The body had been placed in the grave face downward, the head pointing to the south. Two feet above the skeleton were two shining black earthen vases, containing small bits of charcoal, the bones of mammals, birds, and partially consumed corn, and above these "*ollas*" the earth to the surface was filled with pieces of charcoal. Doubtless the remains found in the vases served at a funeral feast prior to the inhumation. We examined very carefully this grave, hoping to find some utensils, ornaments, or weapons, but none rewarded our search. In all of the graves examined the bodies were found in similar positions and under similar circumstances in both arroyas, several of the skeletons being those of children. No information could be obtained as to the probable age of these interments, the present Indians considering them as dating from the time when their ancestors with Moctezuma came from the *north*.

The Coyotero Apaches, according to Dr. W. J. Hoffman, [12] in disposing of their dead, seem to be actuated by the desire to spare themselves any needless trouble, and prepare the defunct and the grave in this manner:

The Coyoteros, upon the death of a member of the tribe, partially wrap up the corpse and deposit it into the cavity left by the removal of a small rock or the stump of a tree. After the body has been crammed into the smallest possible space the rock or stump is again rolled into its former position, when a number of stones are placed around the base to keep out the coyotes. The nearest of kin usually mourn for the period of one month, during that time giving utterance at intervals to the most dismal lamentations, which are apparently sincere. During the day this obligation is frequently neglected or forgotten, but when the mourner is reminded of his duty he renews his howling with evident interest. This custom of mourning for the period of thirty days corresponds to that formerly observed by the Natchez.

Somewhat similar to this rude mode of sepulture is that described in the life of Moses Van Campen, [13] which relates to the Indians formerly inhabiting Pennsylvania:

Directly after, the Indians proceeded to bury those who had fallen in battle, which they did by rolling an old log from its place and laying the body in the hollow thus made, and then heaping upon it a little earth.

As a somewhat curious, if not exceptional, interment, the following account, relating to the Indians of New York, is furnished, by Mr. Franklin B. Hough, who has extracted it from an unpublished journal of the agents of a French company kept in 1794:

CANOE BURIAL IN GROUND.

Saw Indian graves on the plateau of Independence Rock. The Indians plant a stake on the right side of the head of the deceased and bury them in a bark canoe. Their children come every year to bring provisions to the place where their fathers are buried. One of the graves had fallen in, and we observed in the soil some sticks for stretching skins, the remains of a canoe, &c., and the two straps for carrying it, and near the place where the head lay were the traces of a fire which they had kindled for the soul of the deceased to come and warm itself by and to partake of the food deposited near it.

These were probably the Massasauga Indians, then inhabiting the north shore of Lake Ontario, but who were rather intruders here, the country being claimed by the Oneidas.

It is not to be denied that the use of canoes for coffins has occasionally been remarked, for the writer in 1873 removed from the graves at Santa Barbara, California, an entire skeleton which was discovered in a redwood canoe, but it is thought that the individual may have been a noted fisherman, particularly as the implements of his vocation—nets, fish-spears, &c.—were near him, and this burial was only an exemplification of the well-rooted belief common to all Indians, that the spirit in the next world makes use of the same articles as were employed in this one. It should be added that of the many hundreds of skeletons uncovered at Santa Barbara the one mentioned presented the only example of the kind.

Among the Indians of the Mosquito coast, in Central America, canoe burial in the ground, according to Bancroft, was common, and is thus described:

The corpse is wrapped in cloth and placed in one-half of a pitpan which has been cut in two. Friends assemble for the funeral and drown their grief in *mushla*, the women giving vent to their sorrow by dashing themselves on the ground until covered with blood, and inflicting other tortures, occasionally even committing suicide. As it is supposed that the evil spirit seeks to obtain possession of the body, musicians are called in to lull it to sleep while preparations are made for its removal. All at once four naked men, who have disguised themselves with paint so as not to be recognized and punished by *Wulasha*, rush out from a neighboring hut, and, seizing a rope attached to the canoe, drag it into the woods, followed by the music and the crowd. Here the pitpan is lowered into the grave with bow, arrow, spear, paddle, and other implements to serve the departed in the land beyond, then the other half of the boat is placed over the body. A rude hut is constructed over the grave, serving as a receptacle for the choice food, drink, and other articles placed there from time to time by relatives.

STONE GRAVES OR CISTS.

These are of considerable interest, not only from their somewhat rare occurrence, except in certain localities, but from the manifest care taken by the survivors to provide for the dead what they considered a suitable resting place. In their construction they resemble somewhat, in the care that is taken to prevent the earth touching the corpse, the class of graves previously described.

A number of cists have been found in Tennessee, and are thus described by Moses Fiske: [14]

> There are many burying grounds in West Tennessee with regular graves. They dug them 12 or 18 inches deep, placed slabs at the bottom ends and sides, forming a kind of stone coffin, and, after laying in the body, covered it over with earth.

It may be added that, in 1873, the writer assisted at the opening of a number of graves of men of the reindeer period, near Solutré, in France, and they were almost identical in construction with those described by Mr. Fiske, with the exception that the latter were deeper, this, however, may be accounted for if it is considered how great a deposition of earth may have taken place during the many centuries which have elapsed since the burial. Many of the graves explored by the writer in 1875, at Santa Barbara, resembled somewhat cist graves, the bottom and sides of the pit being lined with large flat stones, but there were none directly over the skeletons.

The next account is by Maj. J. W. Powell, the result of his own observation in Tennessee.

> The burial places, or cemeteries are exceedingly abundant throughout the State. Often hundreds of graves may be found on a single hillside. The same people sometimes bury in scattered graves and in mounds— the mounds being composed of a large number of cist graves. The graves are increased by additions from time to time. The additions are sometimes placed above and sometimes at the sides of the others. In the first burials there is a tendency to a concentric system with the feet towards the center, but subsequent burials are more irregular, so that the system is finally abandoned before the place is desired for cemetery purposes.

> Some other peculiarities are of interest. A larger number of interments exhibit the fact that the bodies were placed there before the decay of the flesh, and in many instances collections of bones are buried. Sometimes these bones are placed in some order about the crania, and sometimes in irregular piles, as if the collection of bones had been emptied from a sack. With men, pipes, stone hammers, knives, arrowheads, &c., were usually found, with women, pottery, rude

beads, shells, &c., with children, toys of pottery, beads, curious pebbles, &c.

Sometimes, in the subsequent burials, the side slab of a previous burial was used as a portion of the second cist. All of the cists were covered with slabs.

Dr. Jones has given an exceedingly interesting account of the stone graves of Tennessee, in his volume published by the Smithsonian Institution, to which valuable work [15] the reader is referred for a more detailed account of this mode of burial.

G. K. Gilbert, of the United States Geological Survey, informs the writer that in 1878 he had a conversation with an old Moquis chief as to their manner of burial, which is as follows: The body is placed in a receptacle or cist of stone slabs or wood, in a sitting posture, the hands near the knees, and clasping a stick (articles are buried with the dead), and it is supposed that the soul finds its way out of the grave by climbing up the stick, which is allowed to project above the ground after the grave is filled in.

The Indians of Illinois, on the Saline River, according to George Escoll Sellers, [16] inclosed their dead in cists, the description of which is as follows:

Above this bluff, where the spur rises at an angle of about 30°, it has been terraced and the terrace as well as the crown of the spur have been used as a cemetery; portions of the terraces are still perfect; all the burials appear to have been made in rude stone cists, that vary in size from 13 inches by 3 feet to 2 feet by 4 feet, and from 18 inches to 2 feet deep. They are made of thin-bedded sandstone slabs, generally roughly shaped, but some of them have been edged and squared with considerable care, particularly the covering slabs. The slope below the terraces was thickly strewed with these slabs, washed out as the terraces have worn away, and which have since been carried off for door-steps and hearth-stones. I have opened many of these cists; they nearly all contain fragments of human bones far gone in decay, but I have never succeeded in securing a perfect skull; even the clay vessels that were interred with the dead have disintegrated, the portions remaining being almost as soft and fragile as the bones. Some of the cists that I explored were paved with valves of fresh-water shells, but most generally with the fragments of the great salt-pans, which in every case are so far gone in decay as to have lost the outside markings. This seems conclusively to couple the tenants of these ancient graves with the makers and users of these salt-pans. The great number of graves and the quantity of slabs that have been washed out prove either a dense population or a long occupancy, or both.

W. J. Owsley, of Fort Hall, Idaho, furnishes the writer with a description of the cist graves of Kentucky, which differ somewhat from other accounts, inasmuch as the graves appeared to be isolated.

I remember that when a school-boy in Kentucky, some twenty-five years ago, of seeing what was called "Indian graves," and those that I examined were close to small streams of water, and were buried in a sitting or squatting posture and inclosed by rough, flat stones, and were then buried from 1 to 4 feet from the surface. Those graves which I examined, which examination was not very minute, seemed to be isolated, no two being found in the same locality. When the burials took place I could hardly conjecture, but it must have been, from appearances, from fifty to one hundred years. The bones that I took out on first appearance seemed tolerably perfect, but on short exposure to the atmosphere crumbled, and I was unable to save a specimen. No implements or relics were observed in those examined by me, but I have heard of others who have found such. In that State, Kentucky, there are a number of places where the Indians buried their dead and left mounds of earth over the graves, but I have not examined them myself.   *   *   *

According to Bancroft, [17] the Dorachos, an isthmian tribe of Central America, also followed the cist form of burial.

In Veragua the Dorachos had two kinds of tombs, one for the principal men, constructed with flat stones laid together with much care, and in which were placed costly jars and urns filled with food and wine for the dead. Those for the plebians were merely trenches, in which were deposited some gourds of maize and wine, and the place filled with stones. In some parts of Panama and Darien only the chiefs and lords received funeral rites. Among the common people a person feeling his end approaching either went himself or was led to the woods by his wife, family, or friends, who, supplying him with some cake or ears of corn and a gourd of water, then left him to die alone or to be assisted by wild beasts. Others, with more respect for their dead, buried them in sepulchers made with niches, where they placed maize and wine and renewed the same annually. With some, a mother dying while suckling her infant, the living child was placed at her breast and buried with her, in order that in her future state she might continue to nourish it with her milk.

BURIAL IN MOUNDS.

In view of the fact that the subject of mound-burial is so extensive, and that in all probability a volume by a member of the Bureau of Ethnology may shortly be published, it is not deemed advisable to devote any considerable space to it in this paper, but a few interesting examples may be noted to serve as indications to future observers.

The first to which attention is directed is interesting as resembling cist burial combined with deposition in mounds. The communication is from Prof. F. W. Putnam, curator of the Peabody Museum of Archæology, Cambridge, made to the Boston Society of Natural History, and is published in volume XX of its proceedings, October 15, 1878:

> * * * He then stated that it would be of interest to the members, in connection with the discovery of dolmens in Japan, as described by Professor Morse, to know that within twenty-four hours there had been received at the Peabody Museum a small collection of articles taken from rude dolmens (or chambered barrows, as they would be called in England), recently opened by Mr. E. Curtiss, who is now engaged, under his direction, in exploration for the Peabody Museum.

> These chambered mounds are situated in the eastern part of Clay County, Missouri, and form a large group on both sides of the Missouri River. The chambers are, in the three opened by Mr. Curtiss, about 8 feet square, and from 4½ to 5 feet high, each chamber having a passage-way several feet in length and 2 in width, leading from the southern side and opening on the edge of the mound formed by covering the chamber and passage-way with earth. The walls of the chambered passages were about 2 feet thick, vertical, and well made of stones, which were evenly laid without clay or mortar of any kind. The top of one of the chambers had a covering of large, flat rocks, but the others seem to have been closed over with wood. The chambers were filled with clay which had been burnt, and appeared as if it had fallen in from above. The inside walls of the chambers also showed signs of fire. Under the burnt clay, in each chamber, were found the remains of several human skeletons, all of which had been burnt to

such an extent as to leave but small fragments of the bones, which were mixed with the ashes and charcoal. Mr. Curtiss thought that in one chamber he found the remains of 5 skeletons and in another 13. With these skeletons there were a few flint implements and minute fragments of vessels of clay.

A large mound near the chambered mounds was also opened, but in this no chambers were found. Neither had the bodies been burnt. This mound proved remarkably rich in large flint implements, and also contained well-made pottery and a peculiar "gorget" of red stone. The connection of the people who placed the ashes of their dead in the stone chambers with those who buried their dead in the earth mounds is, of course, yet to be determined.

It is quite possible, indeed probable, that these chambers were used for secondary burials, the bodies having first been cremated.

In the volume of the proceedings already quoted, the same investigator gives an account of other chambered mounds which are, like the preceding, very interesting, the more so as adults only were inhumed therein, children having been buried beneath the dwelling-floors:

Mr. F. W. Putnam occupied the rest of the evening with an account of his explorations of the ancient mounds and burial places in the Cumberland Valley, Tennessee.

The excavations had been carried on by himself, assisted by Mr. Edwin Curtiss, for over two years, for the benefit of the Peabody Museum at Cambridge. During this time many mounds of various kinds had been thoroughly explored, and several thousand of the singular stone graves of the mound builders of Tennessee had been carefully opened.   *   *   *   Mr. Putnam's remarks were illustrated by drawings of several hundred objects obtained from the graves and mounds, particularly to show the great variety of articles of pottery and several large and many unique forms of implements of chipped flint. He also exhibited and explained in detail a map of a walled town of this old nation. This town was situated on the Lundsley estate, in a bend of Spring Creek. The earth embankment, with its accompanying ditch, encircled an area of about 12 acres. Within this inclosure there was one large mound with a flat top, 15 feet high, 130 feet long, and 90 feet wide, which was found not to be a burial mound. Another mound near the large one, about 50 feet in diameter, and only a few feet high, contained 60 human skeletons, each in a carefully-made stone grave, the graves being arranged in two rows, forming the four sides of a square, and in three layers.   *   *   *   The most important discovery he made within the inclosure was that of finding the remains of the houses of the people who lived in this old town. Of them about 70 were traced out and located on the map by Professor Buchanan, of Lebanon, who made the survey for Mr. Putnam. Under the floors of hard clay, which was in places much burnt, Mr. Putnam found the graves of children. As only the bodies of adults had been placed in the one mound devoted to burial, and as nearly every site of a house he explored had from one to four graves of children under the clay floor, he was convinced that it was a regular custom to bury the children in that way. He also found that the children had undoubtedly been treated with affection, as in their small graves were found many of the best pieces of pottery he obtained, and also quantities of shell-beads, several large pearls, and many other objects which were probably the playthings of the little ones while living.[18]

This cist mode of burial is by no means uncommon in Tennessee, as it is frequently mentioned by writers on North American archæology.

The examples which follow are specially characteristic, some of them serving to add strength to the theory that mounds were for the most part used for secondary burial, although intrusions were doubtless common.

Caleb Atwater [19] gives this description of the

BURIAL MOUNDS OF OHIO.

Near the center of the round fort   *   *   *   was a tumulus of earth about 10 feet in height and several rods in diameter at its base. On its eastern side, and extending 6 rods from it, was a semicircular pavement composed of pebbles such as are now found in the bed of the Scioto River, from whence they appear to have been brought. The summit of this tumulus was nearly 30 feet in diameter, and there was a raised way to it, leading from the east, like a modern turnpike. The summit was level. The outline of the semicircular pavement and the walk is still discernible. The earth composing this mound was entirely removed several years since. The writer was present at its removal and carefully examined the contents. It contained—

1st. Two human skeletons, lying on what had been the original surface of the earth.

2d. A great quantity of arrow-heads, some of which were so large as to induce a belief that they were used as spear-heads.

3d. The handle either of a small sword or a huge knife, made of an elk's horn. Around the end where the blade had been inserted was a ferule of silver, which, though black, was not much injured by time. Though the handle showed the hole where the blade had been inserted, yet no iron was found, but an oxyde remained of similar shape and size.

4th. Charcoal and wood ashes on which these articles lay, which were surrounded by several bricks very well burnt. The skeleton appeared to have been burned in a large and very hot fire, which had almost consumed the bones of the deceased. This skeleton was deposited a little to the south of the center of the tumulus; and about 20 feet to the north of it was another, with which were—

5th. A large mirrour about 3 feet in breadth and 1½ inches in thickness. This mirrour was of isinglass (*mica membranacea*), and on it—

6th. A plate of iron which had become an oxyde, but before it was disturbed by the spade resembled a plate of cast iron. The mirrour answered the purpose very well for which it was intended. This skeleton had also been burned like the former, and lay on charcoal and a considerable quantity of wood ashes. A part of the mirrour is in my possession, as well as a piece of brick taken from the spot at the time. The knife or sword handle was sent to Mr. Peal's Museum, at Philadelphia.

To the southwest of this tumulus, about 40 rods from it, is another, more than 90 feet in height, which is shown on the plate representing these works. It stands on a large hill, which appears to be artificial. This must have been the common cemetery, as it contains an immense number of human skeletons of all sizes and ages. The skeletons are laid horizontally, with their heads generally towards the center and the feet towards the outside of the tumulus. A considerable part of this work still stands uninjured, except by time. In it have been found, besides these skeletons, stone axes and knives, and several ornaments, with holes through them, by means of which, with a cord passing through these perforations, they could be worn by their owners. On the south side of this tumulus, and not far from it, was a semicircular fosse, which, when I first saw it, was 6 feet deep. On opening it was discovered at the bottom a great quantity of human bones, which I am inclined to believe were the remains of those who had been slain in some great and destructive battle: first, because they belonged to persons who had attained their full size, whereas in the mound adjoining were found the skeletons of persons of all ages; and, secondly, they were here in the utmost confusion, as if buried in a hurry. May we not conjecture that they belonged to the people who resided in the town, and who were victorious in the engagement? Otherwise they would not have been thus honorably buried in the common cemetery.

Chillicothe mound.—Its perpendicular height was about 15 feet, and the diameter of its base about 60 feet. It was composed of sand and contained human bones belonging to skeletons which were buried in different parts of it. It was not until this pile of earth was removed and the original surface exposed to view that a probable conjecture of its original design could be formed. About 20 feet square of the surface had been leveled and covered with bark. On the center of this lay a human skeleton, over which had been spread a mat manufactured either from weeds or bark. On the breast lay what had been a piece of copper, in the form of a cross, which had now become verdigris. On the breast also lay a stone ornament with two perforations, one near each end, through which passed a string, by means of which it was suspended around the wearer's neck. On this string, which was made of sinews, and very much injured by time, were placed a great many beads made of ivory or bone, for I cannot certainly say which.

* * *

Mounds of stone.—Two such mounds have been described already in the county of Perry. Others have been found in various parts of the country. There is one at least in the vicinity of Licking River, not many miles from Newark. There is another on a branch of Hargus's Creek, a few miles to the northeast of Circleville. There were several not very far from the town of Chillicothe. If these mounds were sometimes used as cemeteries of distinguished persons, they were also used as monuments with a view of perpetuating the recollection of some great transaction or event. In the former not more generally than one or two skeletons are found; in the latter none. These mounds are like those of earth, in form of a cone, composed of small stones on which no marks of tools were visible. In them some of the most interesting articles are found, such as urns, ornaments of copper, heads of spears, &c., of the same metal, as well as medals of copper and pickaxes of horneblende; * * * works of this class, compared with those of earth, are few, and they are none of them as large as the mounds at Grave Creek, in the town of Circleville, which belong to the first class. I saw one of these stone tumuli which had been piled on the surface of the earth on the spot where three skeletons had been buried in stone coffins, beneath the surface. It was situated on the western edge of the hill on which the "walled town" stood, on Paint Creek. The graves appear to have been dug to about the depth of ours in the present times. After the bottom and sides were lined with thin flat stones, the corpses were placed in these graves in an eastern and western direction, and large flat stones were laid over the graves; then the earth which had been dug out of the graves was thrown over them. A huge pile of stones was placed over the whole. It is quite probable, however, that this was a work of our present race of Indians. Such graves are more common in Kentucky than Ohio. No article, except the skeletons, was found in these graves; and the skeletons resembled very much the present race of Indians.

The mounds of Sterling County, Illinois, are described by W. C. Holbrook [20] as follows:

I recently made an examination of a few of the many Indian mounds found on Rock River, about two miles above Sterling, Ill. The first one opened was an oval mound about 20 feet long, 12 feet wide, and 7 feet high. In the interior of this I found a *dolmen* or quadrilateral wall about 10 feet long, 4 feet high, and 4½ feet wide. It had been built of lime-rock from a quarry near by, and was covered with large flat stones. No mortar or cement had been used. The whole structure rested on the surface of the natural soil, the interior of which had been scooped out to enlarge the chamber. Inside of the *dolmen* I found the partly decayed remains of eight human skeletons, two very large teeth of an unknown animal, two fossils, one of which is not found in this place, and a plummet. One of the long bones had been splintered; the fragments had united, but there remained large morbid growths of bone (exostosis) in several places. One of the skulls presented a circular opening about the size of a silver dime. This perforation had been made during life, for the edges had commenced to cicatrize. I later examined three circular mounds, but in them I found no dolmens. The first mound contained three adult human skeletons, a few fragments of the skeleton of a child, the lower maxillary of which indicated it to be about six years old. I also found claws of some carnivorous animal. The surface of the soil had been scooped out and the bodies laid in the excavation and covered with about a foot of earth; fires had then been made upon the grave and the mound afterwards completed. The bones had not been charred. No charcoal was found among the bones, but occurred in abundance in a stratum about one foot above them. Two other mounds, examined at the same time, contain no remains.

Of two other mounds, opened later, the first was circular, about 4 feet high, and 15 feet in diameter at the base, and was situated on an elevated point of land close to the bank of the river. From the top of this mound one might view the country for many miles in almost any direction. On its summit was an oval altar 6 feet long and 4½ wide. It was composed of flat pieces of limestone, which had been burned red, some portions having been almost converted into lime. On and about this altar I found abundance of charcoal. At the sides of the altar were fragments of human bones, some of which had been charred. It was covered by a natural growth of vegetable mold and sod, the thickness of which was about 10 inches. Large trees had once grown in this vegetable mold, but their stumps were so decayed I could not tell with certainty; to what species they belonged. Another large mound was opened which contained nothing.

The next account relates to the grave-mounds near Pensacola, Fla., and was originally published by Dr. George M. Sternberg, surgeon United States Army: [21]

Before visiting the mound I was informed that the Indians were buried in it in an upright position, each one with a clay pot on his head. This idea was based upon some superficial explorations which had been made from time to time by curiosity hunters. Their excavations had, indeed, brought to light pots containing fragments of skulls, but not buried in the position they imagined. Very extensive explorations, made at different times by myself, have shown that only fragments of skulls and of the long bones of the body are to be found in the mound, and that these are commonly associated with earthen pots, sometimes whole, but more frequently broken fragments only. In some instances portions of the skull were placed in a pot, and the long bones were deposited in its immediate vicinity. Again, the pots would contain only sand, and fragments of bones would be found near them. The most successful "find" I made was a whole nest of pots, to the number of half a dozen, all in a good state of preservation, and buried with a fragment of skull, which I take, from its small size, to have been that of a female. Whether this female was thus distinguished above all others buried in the mound by the number of pots deposited with her remains because of her skill in the manufacture of such ware, or by reason of the unusual wealth of her sorrowing husband, must remain a matter of conjecture. I found, altogether, fragments of skullsand thigh-bones belonging to at least fifty individuals, but in no instance did I find anything like a complete skeleton. There were no vertebræ, no ribs, no pelvic bones, and none of the small bones of the hands and feet. Two or three skulls, nearly perfect, were found, but they were so fragile that it was impossible to preserve them. In the majority of instances, only fragments of the frontal and parietal bones were found, buried in pots or in fragments of pots too small to have ever contained a complete skull. The conclusion was irresistible that this was not a burial-place for *the bodies* of deceased Indians, but that the bones had been gathered from some other locality for burial in this mound, or that cremation was practiced before burial, and the fragments of bone not consumed by fire were gathered and deposited in the mound. That the latter supposition is the correct one I deem probable from the fact that in digging in the mound evidences of fire are found in numerous places, but without any regularity as to depth and position. These evidences consist in strata of from one to four inches in thickness, in which the sand is of a dark color and has mixed with it numerous small fragments of charcoal.

My theory is that the mound was built by gradual accretion in the following manner: That when a death occurred a funeral pyre was erected on the mound, upon which the body was placed. That after the body was consumed, any fragments of bones remaining were gathered, placed in a pot, and buried, and that the ashes and cinders were covered by a layer of sand brought from the immediate vicinity for that purpose. This view is further supported by the fact that only the shafts of the long bones are found, the expanded extremities, which would be most easily consumed, having disappeared; also, by the fact that no bones of children were found. Their bones being smaller, and containing a less proportion of earthy matter, would be entirely consumed.   *   *   *

At the Santa Rosa mound the method of burial was different. Here I found the skeletons complete, and obtained nine well-preserved skulls.

* * * The bodies were not, apparently, deposited upon any regular system, and I found no objects of interest associated with the remains. It may be that this was due to the fact that the skeletons found were those of warriors who had fallen in battle in which they had sustained defeat. This view is supported by the fact that they were all males, and that two of the skulls bore marks of ante-mortem injuries which must have been of a fatal character.

Writing of the Choctaws, Bartram, [22] in alluding to the ossuary, or bone-house, mentions that so soon as this is filled a general inhumation takes place, in this manner:

Then the respective coffins are borne by the nearest relatives of the deceased to the place of interment, where they are all piled one upon another in the form of a pyramid, and the conical hill of earth heaped above.

The funeral ceremonies are concluded with the solemnization of a festival called the feast of the dead.

Florian Gianque, of Cincinnati, Ohio, furnishes an account of a somewhat curious mound-burial which had taken place in the Miami Valley of Ohio:

A mound was opened in this locality, some years ago, containing a central corpse in a sitting posture, and over thirty skeletons buried around it in a circle, also in a sitting posture, but leaning against one another, tipped over towards the right, facing inwards. I did not see this opened, but have seen the mounds and many ornaments, awls, &c., said to have been found near the central body. The parties informing me are trustworthy.

As an example of interment, unique, so far as known, and interesting as being *sui generis*, the following description by Dr. J. Mason Spainhour, of Lenoir, N.C., of an excavation made by him March 11, 1871, on the farm of R. V. Michaux, esq., near John's River, in Burke County, N.C., is given. The author bears the reputation of an observer of undoubted integrity, whose facts as given may not be doubted:

EXCAVATION OF AN INDIAN MOUND.

In a conversation with Mr. Michaux on Indian curiosities, he informed me that there was an Indian mound on his farm which was formerly of considerable height, but had gradually been plowed down; that several mounds in the neighborhood had been excavated, and nothing of

50

interest found in them. I asked permission to examine this mound, which was granted, and upon investigation the following facts were revealed:

Upon reaching the place, I sharpened a stick 4 or 5 feet in length and ran it down in the earth at several places, and finally struck a rock about 18 inches below the surface, which, on digging down, was found to be smooth on top, lying horizontally upon solid earth, about 18 inches above the bottom of the grave, 18 inches in length, and 16 inches in width, and from 2 to 3 inches in thickness, with the corners rounded.

Not finding anything under this rock, I then made an excavation in the south of the grave, and soon struck another rock, which, upon examination, proved to be in front of the remains of a human skeleton in a sitting posture. The bones of the fingers of the right hand were resting on this rock, and on the rock near the hand was a small stone about 5 inches long, resembling a tomahawk or Indian hatchet. Upon a further examination many of the bones were found, though in a very decomposed condition, and upon exposure to the air soon crumbled to pieces. The heads of the bones, a considerable portion of the skull, maxillary bones, teeth, neck bones, and the vertebra, were in their proper places, though the weight of the earth above them had driven them down, yet the entire frame was so perfect that it was an easy matter to trace all the bones; the bones of the cranium were slightly inclined toward the east. Around the neck were found coarse beads that seemed to be of some hard substance and resembled chalk. A small lump of red paint about the size of an egg was found near the right side of this skeleton. The sutures of the cranium indicated the subject to have been 25 or 28 years of age, and its top rested about 12 inches below the mark of the plow.

I made a farther excavation toward the west of this grave and found another skeleton, similar to the first, in a sitting posture, facing the east. A rock was on the right, on which the bones of the right hand were resting, and on this rock was a tomahawk which had been about 7 inches in length, but was broken into two pieces, and was much better finished than the first. Beads were also around the neck of this one, but were much smaller and of finer quality than those on the neck of the first. The material, however, seems to be the same. A much larger amount of paint was found by the side of this than the first. The bones indicated a person of large frame, who, I think, was about 50

51

years of age. Everything about this one had the appearance of superiority over the first. The top of the skull was about 6 inches below the mark of the plane.

I continued the examination, and, after diligent search, found nothing at the north side of the grave; but, on reaching the east, found another skeleton, in the same posture as the others, facing the west. On the right side of this was a rock on which the bones of the right hand were resting, and on the rock was also a tomahawk, which had been about 8 inches in length, but was broken into *three* pieces, and was composed of much better material, and better finished than the others. Beads were also found on the neck of this, but much smaller and finer than those of the others. A larger amount of paint than both of the others was found near this one. The top of the cranium had been moved by the plow. The bones indicated a person of 40 years of age.

There was no appearance of hair discovered; besides, the smaller bones were almost entirely decomposed, and would crumble when taken from their bed in the earth. These two circumstances, coupled with the fact that the farm on which this grave was found was the first settled in that part of the country, the date of the first deed made from Lord Granville to John Perkins running back about 150 years (the land still belonging to the descendants of the same family that first occupied it), would prove beyond doubt that it is a very old grave.

The grave was situated due east and west, in size about 9 by 6 feet, the line being distinctly marked by the difference in the color of the soil. It was dug in rich, black loam, and filled around the bodies with white or yellow sand, which I suppose was carried from the river-bank, 200 yards distant. The skeletons approximated the walls of the grave, and contiguous to them was a dark-colored earth, and so decidedly different was this from all surrounding it, both in quality and odor, that the line of the bodies could be readily traced. The odor of this decomposed earth, which had been flesh, was similar to clotted blood, and would adhere in lumps when compressed in the hand.

This was not the grave of the Indian warriors; in those we find pots made of earth or stone, and all the implements of war, for the warrior had an idea that after he arose from the dead he would need, in the "hunting-grounds beyond," his bow and arrow, war-hatchet, and scalping-knife.

The facts set forth will doubtless convince every Mason who will carefully read the account of this remarkable burial that the American Indians were in possession of at least some of the mysteries of our order, and that it was evidently the grave of Masons, and the three highest officers in a Masonic lodge. The grave was situated due east and west; an altar was erected in the center; the south, west, and east were occupied—*the north was not*; implements of authority were near each body. The difference in the quality of the beads, the tomahawks in one, two, and three pieces, and the difference in distance that the bodies were placed from the surface, indicate beyond doubt that these three persons had been buried by Masons, and those, too, that understood what they were doing.

Will some learned Mason unravel this mystery and inform the Masonic world how the Indians obtained so much Masonic information?

The tomahawks, maxillary bones, some of the teeth, beads, and other bones, have been forwarded to the Smithsonian Institution at Washington, D.C., to be placed among the archives of that institution for exhibition, at which place they may be seen.

Should Dr. Spainhour's inferences be incorrect, there is still a remarkable coincidence of circumstances patent to every Mason.

In support of this gentleman's views, attention is called to the description of the *Midawan*—a ceremony of initiation for would-be medicine men—in Schoolcraft's History of the Indian Tribes of the United States, 1855, p. 428, relating to the Sioux and Chippewas. In this account are found certain forms and resemblances which have led some to believe that the Indians possessed a knowledge of Masonry.

BURIAL BENEATH, OR IN CABINS, WIGWAMS, OR HOUSES.

While there is a certain degree of similitude between the above-noted methods and the one to be mentioned subsequently—*lodge* burial—they differ, inasmuch as the latter are examples of surface or aerial burial, and must consequently fall under another caption. The narratives which are now to be given afford a clear idea of the former kinds of burial.

Bartram [23] relates the following regarding the Muscogulges of the Carolinas:

The Muscogulges bury their deceased in the earth; they dig a four-foot, square, deep pit under the cabin, or couch which the deceased laid on in his house, lining the grave with cypress bark, when they place the corpse in a sitting posture, as if it were alive, depositing with him his gun, tomahawk, pipe, and such other matters as he had the greatest value for in his lifetime. His oldest wife, or the queen dowager, has the second choice of his possessions, and the remaining effects are divided among his other wives and children.

According to Bernard Roman, [24] the "funeral customs of the Chickasaws did not differ materially from those of the Muscogulges. They interred the dead as soon as the breath left the body, and beneath the couch in which the deceased expired."

The Navajos of New Mexico and Arizona, a tribe living a considerable distance from the Chickasaws, follow somewhat similar customs, as related by Dr. John Menard, formerly a physician to their agency:

The Navajo custom is to leave the body where it dies, closing up the house or hogan or covering the body with stones or brush. In case the body is removed, it is taken to a cleft in the rocks and thrown in, and stones piled over. The person touching or carrying the body first takes off all his clothes and afterwards washes his body with water before putting them on or mingling with the living. When a body is removed from a house or hogan, the hogan is burned down, and the place in every case abandoned, as the belief is that the devil comes to the place of death and remains where a dead body is. Wild animals frequently (indeed, generally) get the bodies, and it is a very easy matter to pick up skulls and bones around old camping grounds, or where the dead are laid. In case it is not desirable to abandon a place, the sick person is left out in some lone spot protected by brush, where they are either abandoned to their fate or food brought to them until they die. This is done only when all hope is gone. I have found bodies thus left so well inclosed with brush that wild animals were unable to get at them; and one so left to die was revived by a cup of coffee from our house and is still living and well.

Lieut. George E. Ford, Third United States Cavalry, in a personal communication to the writer, corroborates the account given by Dr. Menard, as follows:

This tribe, numbering about 8,000 souls, occupy a reservation in the extreme northwestern corner of New Mexico and Northeastern

Arizona. The funeral ceremonies of the Navajos are of the most simple character. They ascribe the death of an individual to the direct action of *Chinde*, or the devil, and believe that he remains in the vicinity of the dead. For this reason, as soon as a member of the tribe dies a shallow grave is dug within the hogan or dwelling by one of the near male relatives, and into this the corpse is unceremoniously tumbled by the relatives, who have previously protected themselves from the evil influence by smearing their naked bodies with tar from the piñon tree. After the body has thus been disposed of, the hogan (composed of logs and branches of trees covered with earth) is pulled down over it and the place deserted. Should the deceased have no near relatives or was of no importance in the tribe, the formality of digging a grave is dispensed with, the hogan being simply leveled over the body. This carelessness does not appear to arise from want of natural affection for the dead, but fear of the evil influence of *Chinde* upon the surviving relatives causes them to avoid doing anything that might gain for them his ill-will. A Navajo would freeze sooner than make a fire of the logs of a fallen hogan, even though from all appearances it may have been years in that condition. There are no mourning observances other than smearing the forehead and under the eyes with tar, which is allowed to remain until worn off, and then not renewed. The deceased is apparently forgotten, as his name is never spoken by the survivors for fear of giving offense to *Chinde*.

J. L. Burchard, agent to the Round Valley Indians, of California, furnishes an account of burial somewhat resembling that of the Navajos:

When I first came here the Indians would dig a round hole in the ground, draw up the knees of the deceased Indian, and wrap the body into as small a bulk as possible in blankets, tie them firmly with cords, place them in the grave, throw in beads, baskets, clothing, everything owned by the deceased, and often donating much extra; all gathered around the grave wailing most pitifully, tearing their faces with their nails till the blood would run down their cheeks, pull out their hair, and such other heathenish conduct. These burials were generally made under their thatch houses or very near thereto. The house where one died was always torn down, removed, rebuilt, or abandoned. The wailing, talks, &c., were in their own jargon; none else could understand, and they seemingly knew but little of its meaning (if there was any meaning in it); it simply seemed to be the promptings of grief, without sufficient intelligence to direct any ceremony; each seemed to act out his own impulse.

The next account, taken from M. Butel de Dumont, [25] relating to the Paskagoulas and Billoxis of Louisiana, may be considered as an example of burial in houses, although the author of the work was pleased to consider the receptacles as temples.

Les Paskagoulas et les Billoxis n'enterent point leur Chef, lorsqu'il est décédé; mais-ils font sécher son cadavre au feu et à la fumée de façon qu'ils en font un vrai squelette. Après l'avoir réduit en cet état, ils le portent au Temple (car ils en ont un ainsi que les Natchez), et le mettent à la place de son prédécesseur, qu'ils tirent de l'endroit qu'il occupoit, pour le porter avec les corps de leurs autres Chefs dans le fond du Temple où ils sont tous rangés de suite dressés sur leurs pieds comme des statues. A l'égard du dernier mort, il est exposé à l'entrée de ce Temple sur une espèce d'autel ou de table faite de cannes, et couverte d'une natte très-fine travaillée fort proprement en quarreaux rouges et jaunes avec la peau de ces mêmes cannes. Le cadavre du Chef est exposé au milieu de cette table droit sur ses pieds, soutenu par derrière par une longue perche peinte en rouge dont le bout passe au dessus de sa tête, et à laquelle il est attaché par le milieu du corps avec une liane. D'une main il tient un casse-tête ou une petite hache, de l'autre un pipe; et au-dessus de sa tête, est attaché au bout de la perche qui le soutient, le Calumet le plus fameux de tous ceux qui lui ont été présentés pendant sa vie. Du reste cette table n'est guères élevée de terre que d'un demi-pied; mais elle a au moins six pieds de large et dix de longueur.

C'est sur cette table qu'on vient tous les jours servir à manger à ce Chef mort en mettant devant lui des plats de sagamité, du bled grolé ou boucané, &c. C'est-là aussi qu'au commencement de toutes les récoltes ses Sujets vont lui offrir les premiers de tous les fruits qu'ils peuvent recueillir. Tout ce qui lui est présenté de la sorte reste sur cette table; et comme la porte de ce Temple est toujours ouverte, qu'il n'y a personne préposé pour y veiller, que par conséquent y entre qui veut, et que d'ailleurs il est éloigné du Village d'un grand quart de lieue, il arrive que ce sont ordinairement des Etrangers, Chasseurs ou Sauvages, qui profitent de ces mets et de ces fruits, ou qu'ils sont consommés par les animaux. Mais cela est égal à ces sauvages; et moins il en reste lorsqu'ils retournent le lendemain, plus ils sont dans la joie, disant que leur Chef a bien mangé, et que par conséquent il est content d'eux quoiqu'il les ait abandonnés. Pour leur ouvrir les yeux sur l'extravagance de cette pratique, on a beau leur représenter ce qu'ils ne peuvent s'empêcher de voir eux-mêmes, que ce n'est point ce mort qui mange; ils répondent que si ce n'est pas lui, c'est toujours lui au moins qui offre à qui il lui plaît ce qui a été mis sur la table; qu'après tout c'étoit là la pratique de leur père, de leur mère, de leurs parens; qu'ils n'ont pas plus d'esprit qu'eux, et qu'ils ne sauroient mieux faire que de suivre leur example.

C'est aussi devant cette table, que pendant quelques mois la veuve du Chef, ses enfans, ses plus proches parens, viennent de tems en tems lui rendre visite et lui faire leur harangue, comme s'il étoit en état de les entendre. Les uns lui demandent pourquoi il s'est laissé mourir avant eux? d'autres lui disent que s'il est mort ce n'est point leur faute; que c'est lui même qui s'est tué par telle débauche on par tel effort; enfin s'il y a eu quelque défaut dans son gouvernement, on prend ce tems-là pour le lui reprocher. Cependant ils finissent toujours leur harangue, en lui disant de n'être pas fâché contre eux, de bien manger, et qu'ils auront toujours bien soin de lui.

Another example of burial in houses may be found in vol. vi of the publications of the Hakluyt Society, 1849, p. 89, taken from Strachey's Virginia. It is given more as a curious narrative of an early writer on American ethnology than for any intrinsic value it may possess as a truthful relation of actual events. It relates to the Indians of Virginia:

Within the chauncell of the temple, by the Okens, are the cenotaphies or the monuments of their kings, whose bodyes, so soon as they be dead, they embowell, and, scraping the flesh from off the bones, they dry the same upon hurdells into ashes, which they put into little potts (like the anncyent urnes): the annathomy of the bones they bind together or case up in leather, hanging braceletts, or chaines of copper, beads, pearle, or such like, as they used to wear about most of their joints and neck, and so repose the body upon a little scaffold (as upon a tomb), laying by the dead bodies' feet all his riches in severall basketts, his apook, and pipe, and any one toy, which in his life he held most deare in his fancy; their inwards they stuff with pearle, copper, beads, and such trash, sowed in a skynne, which they overlapp againe very carefully in whit skynnes one or two, and the bodyes thus dressed lastly they rowle in matte, as for wynding sheets, and so lay them orderly one by one, as they dye in their turnes, upon an arche standing (as aforesaid) for the tomb, and thes are all the ceremonies we yet can learne that they give unto their dead. We heare of no sweet oyles or oyntments that they use to dresse or chest their dead bodies with; albeit they want not of the pretious rozzin running out of the great cedar, wherewith in the old time they used to embalme dead bodies, washing them in the oyle and licoure thereof. Only to the priests the care of these temples and holy interments are committed, and these temples are to them as solitary Asseteria colledged or ministers to exercise themselves in contemplation, for they are seldome out of them, and therefore often lye in them and maynteyne contynuall fier in the same, upon a hearth somewhat neere the east end.

For their ordinary burialls they digg a deepe hole in the earth with sharpe stakes, and the corps being lapped in skynns and matts with their jewells, they laye uppon sticks in the ground, and soe cover them with earth; the buryall ended, the women (being painted all their faces with black coale and oyle) do sitt twenty-four howers in their howses, mourning and lamenting by turnes, with such yelling and howling as may expresse their great passions.

While this description brings the subject under the head before given—house burial—at the same time it might also afford an example of embalmment or mummifying.

Figure 1 may be referred to as a probable representation of the temple or charnel-house described.

The modes of burial described in the foregoing accounts are not to be considered rare; for among certain tribes in Africa similar practices prevailed. For instance, the Bari of Central Africa, according to the Rev. J. G. Wood, [26] bury their dead within the inclosure of the home-stead, fix a pole in the ground, and fasten to it certain emblems. The Apingi, according to the same author, permit the corpse to remain in its dwelling until it falls to pieces. The bones are then collected and deposited on the ground a short distance from the village. The Latookas bury within the inclosure of a man's house, although the bones are subsequently removed, placed in an earthen jar, and deposited outside the village. The Kaffirs bury their head-men within the cattle inclosure, the graves of the common people being made outside, and the Bechuanas follow the same general plan.

The following description of Damara burial, from the work quoted above (p. 314), is added as containing an account of certain details which resemble somewhat those followed by North American Indians. In the narrative it will be seen that house burial was followed only if specially desired by the expiring person:

When a Damara chief dies, he is buried in rather a peculiar fashion. As soon as life is extinct—some say even before the last breath is drawn —the bystanders break the spine by a blow from a large stone. They then unwind the long rope that encircles the loins, and lash the body together in a sitting posture, the head being bent over the knees. Ox-hides are then tied over it, and it is buried with its face to the north, as already described when treating of the Bechuanas. Cattle are then slaughtered in honor of the dead chief, and over the grave a post is erected, to which the skulls and hair are attached as a trophy. The bow, arrows, assagai, and clubs of the deceased are hung on the same post. Large stones are pressed into the soil above and around the grave, and a large pile of thorns is also heaped over it, in order to keep off the hyenas, who would be sure to dig up and devour the body before the following day. The grave of a Damara chief is represented on page 302. Now and then a chief orders that his body shall be left in his own house, in which case it is laid on an elevated platform, and a strong fence of thorns and stakes built round the hut.

The funeral ceremonies being completed, the new chief forsakes the place and takes the whole of the people under his command. He remains at a distance for several years, during which time he wears the sign of mourning, i.e., a dark-colored conical cap, and round the neck a thong, to the ends of which are hung two small pieces of ostrich-shell. When the season of mourning is over, the tribe return, headed by the chief, who goes to the grave of his father, kneels over it, and whispers that he has returned, together with the cattle and wives which his father gave him. He then asks for his parent's aid in all his undertakings, and from that moment takes the place which his father filled before him. Cattle are then slaughtered, and a feast held to the memory of the dead chief and in honor of the living one, and each person present partakes of the meat, which is distributed by the chief himself. The deceased chief symbolically partakes of the banquet. A couple of twigs cut from the tree of the particular eanda to which the deceased belonged are considered as his representative, and with this emblem each piece of meat is touched before the guests consume it. In like manner, the first pail of milk that is drawn is taken to the grave and poured over it.

CAVE BURIAL.

Natural or artificial holes in the ground, caverns, and fissures in rocks have been used as places of deposit for the dead since the earliest periods of time, and are used up to the present day by not only the American Indians, but by peoples noted for their mental elevation and civilization, our cemeteries furnishing numerous specimens of artificial or partly artificial caves. As to the motives which have actuated this mode of burial, a discussion would be out of place at this time, except as may incidentally relate to our own Indians, who, so far as can be ascertained, simply adopt caves as ready and convenient resting places for their deceased relatives and friends.

In almost every State in the Union burial caves have been discovered, but as there is more or less of identity between them, a few illustrations will serve the purpose of calling the attention of observers to the subject.

While in the Territory of Utah, in 1872, the writer discovered a natural cave not far from the House Range of mountains, the entrance to which resembled the shaft of a mine. In this the Gosi-Ute Indians had deposited their dead, surrounded with different articles, until it was quite filled up; at least it so appeared from the cursory examination made, limited time preventing a careful exploration. In the fall of the same year another cave was heard of, from an Indian guide, near the Nevada border, in the same Territory, and an attempt made to explore it, which failed for reasons to be subsequently given. This Indian, a Gosi-Ute, who was questioned regarding the funeral ceremonies of his tribe, informed the writer that not far from the very spot where the party were encamped, was a large cave in which he had himself assisted in placing dead members of his tribe. He described it in detail and drew a rough diagram of its position and appearance within. He was asked if an entrance could be effected, and replied that he thought not, as some years previous his people had stopped up the narrow entrance to prevent game from seeking a refuge in its vast vaults, for he asserted that it was so large and extended so far under ground that no man knew its full extent. In consideration, however, of a very liberal bribe, after many refusals, he agreed to act as guide. A rough ride of over an hour and the desired spot was reached. It was found to be almost upon the apex of a small mountain apparently of volcanic origin, for the hole which was pointed out appeared to have been the vent of the crater. This entrance was irregularly circular in form and descended at an angle. As the Indian had stated, it was completely stopped up with large stones and roots of sage brash, and it was only after six hours of uninterrupted, faithful labor that the attempt to explore was abandoned. The guide was asked if many bodies were therein, and replied "Heaps, heaps," moving the hands upwards as far they could be stretched. There is no reason to doubt the accuracy of the information received, as it was voluntarily imparted.

In a communication received from Dr. A. J. McDonald, physician to the Los Pinos Indian Agency, Colorado, a description is given of crevice or rock-fissure burial, which follows:

As soon as death takes place the event is at once announced by the medicine man, and without loss of time the squaws are busily engaged in preparing the corpse for the grave. This does not take long; whatever articles of clothing may have been on the body at the time of death are not removed. The dead man's limbs are straightened out, his weapons of war laid by his side, and his robes and blankets wrapped securely and snugly around him, and now everything is ready for burial. It is the custom to secure if possible, for the purpose of wrapping up the corpse, the robes and blankets in which the Indian died. At the same time that the body is being fitted for internment, the squaws having immediate care of it, together with all the other squaws in the neighborhood, keep up a continued chant or dirge, the dismal cadence of which may, when the congregation of women is large, be heard for quite a long distance. The death song is not a mere inarticulate howl of distress; it embraces expressions eulogistic in character, but whether or not any particular formula of words is adopted on such occasion is a question which I am unable, with the materials at my disposal, to determine with any degree of certainty.

The next duty falling to the lot of the squaws is that of placing the dead man on a horse and conducting the remains to the spot chosen for burial. This is in the cleft of a rock, and, so far as can be ascertained, it has always been customary among the Utes to select sepulchers of this character. From descriptions given by Mr. Harris, who has several times been fortunate enough to discover remains, it would appear that no superstitious ideas are held by this tribe with respect to the position in which the body is placed, the space accommodation of the sepulcher probably regulating this matter; and from the same source I learn that it is not usual to find the remains of more than one Indian deposited in one grave. After the body has been received into the cleft, it is well covered with pieces of rock, to protect it against the ravages of wild animals. The chant ceases, the squaws disperse, and the burial ceremonies are at an end. The men during all this time have not been idle, though they have in no way participated in the preparation of the body, have not joined the squaws in chanting praises to the memory of the dead, and have not even as mere spectators attended the funeral, yet they have had their duties to perform. In conformity with a long-established custom, all the personal property of the deceased is immediately destroyed. His horses and his cattle are shot, and his wigwam, furniture, &c., burned. The performance of this part of the ceremonies is assigned to the men; a duty quite in accord with their taste and inclinations. Occasionally the destruction of horses and other properly is of considerable magnitude, but usually this is not the case, owing to a practice existing with them of distributing their property among their children while they are of a very tender age, retaining to themselves only what is necessary to meet every-day requirements.

The widow "goes into mourning" by smearing her face with a substance composed of pitch and charcoal. The application is made but once, and is allowed to remain on until it wears off. This is the only mourning observance of which I have any knowledge.

The ceremonies observed on the death of a female are the same as those in the case of a male, except that no destruction of property takes place, and of course no weapons are deposited with the corpse. Should a youth die while under the superintendence of white men, the Indians will not as a role have anything to do with the interment of the body. In a case of the kind which occurred at this agency some time ago, the squaws prepared the body in the usual manner; the men of the tribe selected a spot for the burial, and the employee at the agency, after digging a grave and depositing the corpse therein, filled it up according to the fashion of civilized people, and then at the request of the Indians rolled large fragments of rocks on top. Great anxiety was exhibited by the Indians to have the employes perform the service as expeditiously as possible.

Within the past year Ouray, the Ute chief living at the Los Pinos agency, died and was buried, so far as could be ascertained, in a rock fissure or cave 7 or 8 miles from the agency.

An interesting cave in Calaveras County, California, which had been used for burial purposes, is thus described by Prof. J. D. Whitney:[27]

> The following is an account of the cave from which the skulls, now in the Smithsonian collection, were taken: It is near the Stanislaus River, in Calaveras County, on a nameless creek, about two miles from Abbey's Ferry, on the road to Vallicito, at the house of Mr. Robinson. There were two or three persons with me, who had been to the place before and knew that the skulls in question were taken from it. Their visit was some ten years ago, and since that the condition of things in the cave has greatly changed. Owing to some alteration in the road, mining operations, or some other cause which I could not ascertain, there has accumulated on the formerly clean stalagmitic floor of the cave a thickness of some 20 feet of surface earth that completely conceals the bottom, and which could not be removed without considerable expense. This cave is about 27 feet deep at the mouth and 40 to 50 feet at the end, and perhaps 30 feet in diameter. It is the general opinion of those who have noticed this cave and saw it years ago that it was a burying-place of the present Indians. Dr. Jones said he found remains of bows and arrows and charcoal with the skulls he obtained, and which were destroyed at the time the village of Murphy's was burned. All the people spoke of the skulls as lying on the surface and not as buried in the stalagmite.

The next description of cave burial, by W. H. Dall, [28] is so remarkable that it seems worthy of admittance to this paper. It relates probably to the Innuits of Alaska.

> The earliest remains of man found in Alaska up to the time of writing I refer to this epoch [Echinus layer of Dall]. There are some crania found by us in the lowermost part of the Amaknak cave and a cranium obtained at Adakh, near the anchorage in the Bay of Islands. These were deposited in a remarkable manner, precisely similar to that adopted by most of the continental Innuit, but equally different from the modern Aleut fashion. At the Amaknak cave we found what at first appeared to be a wooden inclosure, but which proved to be made of the very much decayed supra-maxillary bones of some large cetacean. These were arranged so as to form a rude rectangular

inclosure covered over with similar pieces of bone. This was somewhat less than 4 feet long, 2 feet wide, and 18 inches deep. The bottom was formed of flat pieces of stone. Three such were found close together, covered with and filled by an accumulation of fine vegetable and organic mold. In each was the remains of a skeleton in the last stages of decay. It had evidently been tied up in the Innuit fashion to get it into its narrow house, but all the bones, with the exception of the skull, were minced to a soft paste, or even entirely gone. At Adakh a fancy prompted me to dig into a small knoll near the ancient shell-heap, and here we found, in a precisely similar sarcophagus, the remains of a skeleton, of which also only the cranium retained sufficient consistency to admit of preservation. This inclosure, however, was filled with a dense peaty mass not reduced to mold, the result of centuries of sphagnous growth, which had reached a thickness of nearly 2 feet above the remains. When we reflect upon the well-known slowness of this kind of growth in these northern regions, attested by numerous Arctic travelers, the antiquity of the remains becomes evident.

It seems beyond doubt that in the majority of cases, especially as regards the caves of the Western States and Territories, the interments were primary ones, and this is likewise true of many of the caverns of Ohio, Indiana, and Kentucky, for in the three States mentioned many mummies have been found, but it is also likely that such receptacles were largely used as places of secondary deposits. The many fragmentary skeletons and loose bones found seem to strengthen this view.

EMBALMMENT OR MUMMIFICATION.

Following and in connection with cave burial, the subject of mummifying or embalming the dead may be taken up, as most specimens of the kind have generally been found in such repositories.

It might be both interesting and instructive to search out and discuss the causes which have led many nations or tribes to adopt certain processes with a view to prevent that return to dust which all flesh must sooner or later experience, but the necessarily limited scope of this work precludes more than a brief mention of certain theories advanced by writers of note, and which relate to the ancient Egyptians. Possibly at the time the Indians of America sought to preserve their dead from decomposition, some such ideas may have animated them, but on this point no definite information has been procured. In the final volume an effort will be made to trace out the origin of mummification among the Indians and aborigines of this continent.

The Egyptians embalmed, according to Cassien, because during the time of the annual inundation no interments could take place, but it is more than likely that this hypothesis is entirely fanciful. It is said by others they believed that so long as the body was preserved from corruption the soul remained in it. Herodotus states that it was to prevent bodies from becoming a prey to animal voracity. "They did not inter them," says he, "for fear of their being eaten by worms; nor did they burn, considering fire as a ferocious beast, devouring everything which it touched." According to Diodorus of Sicily, embalmment originated in filial piety and respect. De Maillet, however, in his tenth letter on Egypt, attributes it entirely to a religious belief, insisted upon by the wise men and priests, who taught their disciples that after a certain number of cycles, of perhaps thirty or forty thousand years, the entire universe became as it was at birth, and the souls of the dead returned into the same bodies in which they had lived, provided that the body remained free from corruption, and that sacrifices were freely offered as oblations to the manes of the deceased. Considering the great care taken to preserve the dead, and the ponderously solid nature of the Egyptian tombs, it is not surprising that this theory has obtained many believers. M. Gannal believes embalmment to have been suggested by the affectionate sentiments of our nature—a desire to preserve as long as possible the mortal remains of loved ones; but MM. Volney and Pariset think it was intended to obviate, in hot climates especially, danger from pestilence, being primarily a cheap and simple process, elegance and luxury coming later; and the Count de Caylus states the idea of embalmment was derived from the finding of desiccated bodies which the burning sands of Egypt had hardened and preserved. Many other suppositions have arisen, but it is thought the few given above are sufficient to serve as an introduction to embalmment in North America.

From the statements of the older writers on North American Indians, it appears that mummifying was resorted to, among certain tribes of Virginia, the Carolinas, and Florida, especially for people of distinction, the process in Virginia for the kings, according to Beverly, [29] being as follows:

The *Indians* are religious in preserving the Corpses of their Kings and

Rulers after Death, which they order in the following manner: First, they neatly flay off the Skin as entire as they can, slitting it only in the Back; then they pick all the Flesh off from the Bones as clean as possible, leaving the Sinews fastned to the Bones, that they may preserve the Joints together; then they dry the Bones in the Sun, and put them into the Skin again, which in the mean time has been kept from drying or shrinking; when the Bones are placed right in the Skin, they nicely fill up the Vacuities, with a very fine white Sand. After this they sew up the Skin again, and the Body looks as if the Flesh had not been removed. They take care to keep the Skin from shrinking, by the help of a little Oil or Grease, which saves it also from Corruption. The Skin being thus prepar'd, they lay it in an apartment for that purpose, upon a large Shelf rais'd above the Floor. This Shelf is spread with Mats, for the Corpse to rest easy on, and skreened with the same, to keep it from the Dust. The Flesh they lay upon Hurdles in the Sun to dry, and when it is thoroughly dried, it is sewed up in a Basket, and set at the Feet of the Corpse, to which it belongs. In this place also they set up a *Quioccos*, or Idol, which they believe will be a Guard to the Corpse. Here Night and Day one or the other of the Priests must give his Attendance, to take care of the dead Bodies. So great an Honour and Veneration have these ignorant and unpolisht People for their Princes even after they are dead.

It should be added that, in the writer's opinion, this account and others like it are somewhat apocryphal, and it has been copied and recopied a score of times.

According to Pinkerton, [30] who took the account from Smith's Virginia, the Werowance of Virginia preserved their dead as follows:

In their Temples they have his [their chief God, the Devil's] image euill favouredly carved, and then painted and adorned with chaines of copper, and beads, and covered with a skin, in such manner as the deformitie may well suit with such a God. By him is commonly the sepulchre of their Kings. Their bodies are first bowelled, then dried upon hurdles till they be very dry, and so about the most of their ioynts and necke they hang bracelets, or chaines of copper, pearle, and such like, as they use to wear. Their inwards they stuffe with copper beads, hatchets, and such trash. Then lappe they them very carefully in white skins, and so rowle them in mats for their winding-sheets. And in the Tombe, which is an arch made of mats, they lay them orderly. What remaineth of this kind of wealth their Kings have, they set at their feet in baskets. These temples and bodies are kept by their Priests.

For their ordinary burials, they dig a deepe hole in the earth with sharpe stakes, and the corpse being lapped in skins and mats with their Jewels they lay them upon stickes in the ground, and so cover them with earth. The buriale ended, the women being painted all their faces with blacke cole and oyle doe sit twenty-foure houres in the houses mourning and lamenting by turnes with such yelling and howling as may expresse their great passions.   *   *   *

Upon the top of certain red sandy hills in the woods there are three great houses filled with images of their Kings and devils and the tombes of their predecessors. Those houses are near sixty feet in length, built harbourwise after their building. This place they count so holey as that but the priests and Kings dare come into them; nor the savages dare not go up the river in boates by it, but that they solemnly cast some piece of copper, white beads or pocones into the river for feare their Okee should be offended and revenged of them.

They think that their Werowances and priests which they also esteeme quiyough-cosughs, when they are deade doe goe beyond the mountains towards the setting of the sun, and ever remain there in form of their Okee, with their bedes paynted rede with oyle and pocones, finely trimmed with feathers, and shall have beads, hatchets, copper, and tobacco, doing nothing but dance and sing with all their predecessors. But the common people they suppose shall not live after deth, but rot in their graves like dede dogges.

This is substantially the same account as has been given on a former page, the verbiage differing slightly, and the remark regarding truthfulness will apply to it as well as to the other.

Figure 1 may again be referred to as an example of the dead-house described.

The Congaree or Santee Indians of South Carolina, according to Lawson, used a process of partial embalmment, as will be seen from the subjoined extract from Schoolcraft; [31] but instead of laying away the remains in caves, placed them in boxes supported above the ground by crotched sticks.

The manner of their interment is thus: A mole or pyramid of earth is raised, the mould thereof being worked very smooth and even, sometimes higher or lower according to the dignity of the person whose monument it is. On the top thereof is an umbrella, made ridgeways, like the roof of a house. This in supported by nine stakes or small posts, the grave being about 6 to 8 feet in length and 4 feet in breadth, about which is hung gourds, feathers, and other such like trophies, placed there by the dead man's relations in respect to him in the grave. The other parts of the funeral rites are thus: As soon as the party is dead they lay the corpse upon a piece of bark in the sun, seasoning or embalming it with a small root beaten to powder, which looks as red as vermillion; the same is mixed with bear's oil to beautify the hair. After the carcass has laid a day or two in the sun they remove it and lay it upon crotches cut on purpose for the support thereof from the earth; then they anoint it all over with the aforementioned ingredients of the powder of this root and bear's oil. When it is so done they cover it over very exactly with the bark or pine of the cypress tree to prevent any rain to fall upon it, sweeping the ground very clean all about it. Some of his nearest of kin brings all the temporal estate he was possessed of at his death, as guns, bows and arrows, beads, feathers, match-coat, &c. This relation is the chief mourner, being clad in moss, with a stick in his hand, keeping a mournful ditty for three or four days, his face being black with the smoke of pitch pine mixed with bear's oil. All the while he tells the dead man's relations and the rest of the spectators who that dead person was, and of the great feats performed in his lifetime, all that he speaks tending to the praise of the defunct. As soon as the flesh grows mellow and will cleave from the bone they get it off and burn it, making the bones very clean, then anoint them with the ingredients aforesaid, wrapping up the skull (very carefully) in a cloth artificially woven of opossum's hair. The bones they carefully preserve in a wooden box, every year oiling and cleansing them. By these means they preserve them for many ages, that you may see an Indian in possession of the bones of his grandfather or some of his relations of a longer antiquity. They have other sorts of tombs, as when an Indian is slain in that very place they make a heap of stones (or sticks where stones are not to be found); to this memorial every Indian that passes by adds a stone to augment the heap in respect to the deceased hero. The Indians make a roof of light wood or pitch-pine over the graves of the more distinguished, covering it with bark and then with earth, leaving the body thus in a subterranean vault until the flesh quits the bones. The bones are then taken up, cleaned, jointed, clad in white-dressed deerskins, and laid away in the *Quiogozon*, which is the royal tomb or burial-place of their kings and war-captains, being a more magnificent cabin reared at the public expense. This Quiogozon is an object of veneration, in which the writer says he has known the king, old men, and conjurers to spend several days with their idols and dead kings, and into which he could never gain admittance.

Another class of mummies are those which have been found in the saltpetre and other caves of Kentucky, and it is still a matter of doubt with archæologists whether any special pains were taken to preserve these bodies, many believing that the impregnation of the soil with certain minerals would account for the condition in which the specimens were found. Charles Wilkins [32] thus describes one:

> * * * An exsiccated body of a female [33] * * * was found at the depth of about 10 feet from the surface of the cave bedded in clay strongly impregnated with nitre, placed in a sitting posture, incased in broad stones standing on their edges, with a flat atone covering the whole. It was enveloped in coarse clothes,
> * * * the whole wrapped in deer-skins, the hair of which was shaved off in the manner in which the Indians prepare them for market. Enclosed in the stone coffin were the working utensils, beads, feathers, and other ornaments of dress which belonged to her.

The next description is by Dr. Samuel L. Mitchill. [34*]

AUG. 24TH, 1815.

DEAR SIR: I offer you some observations on a curious piece of American antiquity now in New York. It is a human body: found in one of the limestone caverns of Kentucky. It is a perfect desiccation; all the fluids are dried up. The skin, bones, and other firm parts are in a state of entire preservation. I think it enough to have puzzled Bryant and all the archæologists.

This was found in exploring a calcareous cave in the neighborhood of Glasgow for saltpetre.

These recesses, though under ground, are yet dry enough to attract and retain the nitrick acid. It combines with lime and potash; and probably the earthy matter of these excavations contains a good proportion of calcareous carbonate. Amidst them drying and antiseptick ingredients, it may be conceived that putrefaction would be stayed, and the solids preserved from decay. The outer envelope of the body is a deer-skin, probably dried in the usual way, and perhaps softened before its application by rubbing. The next covering is a deer's skin, whose hair had been cut away by a sharp instrument resembling a batter's knife.

The remnant of the hair and the gashes in the skin nearly resemble a sheared pelt of beaver. The next wrapper is of cloth made of twine doubled and twisted. But the thread does not appear to have been formed by the wheel, nor the web by the loom. The warp and filling seem to have been crossed and knotted by an operation like that of the fabricks of the northwest coast, and of the Sandwich Islands. Such a botanist as the lamented Muhlenbergh could determine the plant which furnished the fibrous material.

The innermost tegument is a mantle of cloth, like the preceding, but furnished with large brown feathers, arranged and fashioned with great art, so as to be capable of guarding the living wearer from wet and cold. The plumage is distinct and entire, and the whole bears a near similitude to the feathery cloaks now worn by the nations of the northwestern coast of America. A Wilson might tell from what bird they were derived.

The body is in a squatting posture, with the right arm reclining forward, and its hand encircling the right leg. The left arm hangs down, with its hand inclined partly under the seat. The individual, who was a male, did not probably exceed the age of fourteen at his death. There is near the occiput a deep and extensive fracture of the skull, which probably killed him. The skin has sustained little injury; it is of a dusky colour, but the natural hue cannot be decided with exactness, from its present appearance. The scalp, with small exceptions, is covered with sorrel or foxey hair. The teeth are white and sound. The hands and feet, in their shrivelled state, are slender and delicate. All this is worthy the investigation of our acute and perspicacious colleague, Dr. Holmes.

There is nothing bituminous or aromatic in or about the body, like the Egyptian mummies, nor are there bandages around any part. Except the several wrappers, the body is totally naked. There is no sign of a suture or incision about the belly; whence it seems that the viscera were not removed.

It may now be expected that I should offer some opinion as to the antiquity and race of this singular exsiccation.

First, then, I am satisfied that it does not belong to that class of white men of which we are members.

2dly. Nor do I believe that it ought to be referred to the bands of

Spanish adventurers, who, between the years 1500 and 1600, rambled up the Mississippi, and along its tributary streams. But on this head I should like to know the opinion of my learned and sagacious friend, Noah Webster.

3dly. I am equally obliged to reject the opinion that it belonged to any of the tribes of aborigines, now or lately inhabiting Kentucky.

4thly. The mantle of the feathered work, and the mantle of twisted threads, so nearly resemble the fabricks of the indigines of Wakash and the Pacifick Islands, that I refer this individual to that era of time, and that generation of men, which preceded the Indians of the Green River, and of the place where these relicks were found. This conclusion is strengthened by the consideration that such manufactures are not prepared by the actual and resident red men of the present day. If the Abbe Clavigero had had this case before him, he would have thought of the people who constructed those ancient forts and mounds, whose exact history no man living can give. But I forbear to enlarge; my intention being merely to manifest my respect to the society for having enrolled me among its members, and to invite the attention of its Antiquarians to further inquiry on a subject of such curiousity.

With respect, I remain yours,

SAMUEL L. MITCHILL.

It would appear, from recent researches on the Northwest coast, that the natives of that region embalmed their dead with much care, as may be seen from the work recently published by W. H. Dall, [35] the description of the mummies being as follows:

We found the dead disposed of in various ways; first, by interment in their compartments of the communal dwelling, as already described; second, by being laid on a rude platform of drift-wood or stones in some convenient rock shelter. These lay on straw and moss, covered by matting, and rarely have either implements, weapons, or carvings associated with them. We found only three or four specimens in all in these places, of which we examined a great number. This was apparently the more ancient form of disposing of the dead, and one which more recently was still pursued in the case of poor or unpopular individuals.

Lastly, in comparatively modern times, probably within a few centuries, and up to the historic period (1740), another mode was adopted for the wealthy, popular, or more distinguished class. The bodies were eviscerated, cleansed from fatty matters in running water, dried, and usually placed in suitable cases in wrappings of fur and fine grass matting. The body was usually doubled up into the smallest compass, and the mummy case, especially in the case of children, was usually suspended (so as not to touch the ground) in some convenient rock shelter. Sometimes, however, the prepared body was placed in a lifelike position, dressed and armed. They were placed as if engaged in some congenial occupation, such as hunting, fishing, sewing, &c. With them were also placed effigies of the animals they were pursuing, while the hunter was dressed in his wooden armor and provided with an enormous mask all ornamented with feathers, and a countless variety of wooden pendants, colored in gay patterns. All the carvings were of wood, the weapons even were only fac-similes in wood of the original articles. Among the articles represented were drums, rattles, dishes, weapons, effigies of men, birds, fish, and animals, wooden armor of rods or scales of wood, and remarkable masks, so arranged that the wearer when erect could only see the ground at his feet. These were worn at their religious dances from an idea that a spirit which was supposed to animate a temporary idol was fatal to whoever might look upon it while so occupied. An extension of the same idea led to the masking of those who had gone into the land of spirits.

The practice of preserving the bodies of those belonging to the whaling class—a custom peculiar to the Kadiak Innuit—has erroneously been confounded with the one now described. The latter included women as well as men, and all those whom the living desired particularly to honor. The whalers, however, only preserved the bodies of males, and they were not associated with the paraphernalia of those I have described. Indeed, the observations I have been able to make show the bodies of the whalers to have been preserved with stone weapons and actual utensils instead of effigies, and with the meanest apparel, and no carvings of consequence. These details, and those of many other customs and usages of which the shell heaps bear no testimony   *   *   *   do not come within my line.

Figure 5, copied from Dall, represents the Alaskan mummies.

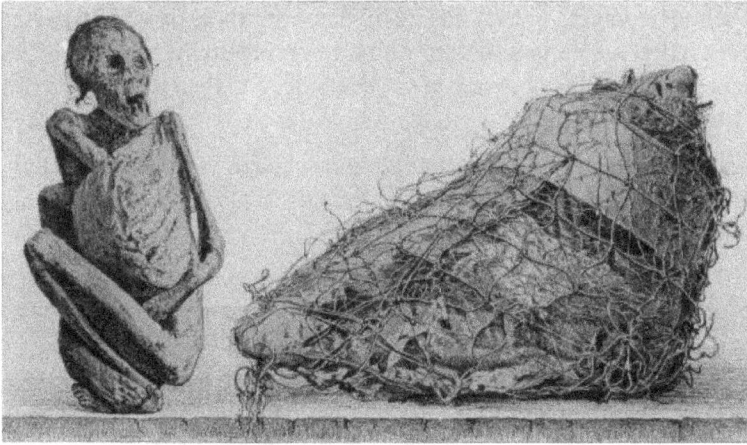

F$_{IG}$. 5.—Alaskan Mummies.

Martin Sauer, secretary to Billings' Expedition, [36] speaks of the Aleutian Islanders embalming their dead, as follows:

They pay respect, however, to the memory of the dead, for they embalm the bodies of the men with dried moss and grass; bury them in their best attire, in a sitting posture, in a strong box, with their darts and instruments; and decorate the tomb with various coloured mats, embroidery, and paintings. With women, indeed, they use less ceremony. A mother will keep a dead child thus embalmed in their hut for some months, constantly wiping it dry; and they bury it when it begins to smell, or when they get reconciled to parting with it.

Regarding these same people, a writer in the San Francisco Bulletin gives this account:

The schooner William Sutton, belonging to the Alaska Commercial Company, has arrived from the seal islands of the company with the mummified remains of Indians who lived on an island north of Ounalaska one hundred and fifty years ago. This contribution to science was secured by Captain Henning, an agent of the company who has long resided at Ounalaska. In his transactions with the Indians he learned that tradition among the Aleuts assigned Kagamale, the island in question, as the last resting-place of a great chief, known as Karkhayahouchak. Last year the captain was in the neighborhood of Kagamale in quest of sea-otter and other furs, and he bore up for the island, with the intention of testing the truth of the tradition he had heard. He had more difficulty in entering the cave than in finding it,

73

his schooner having to beat on and off shore for three days. Finally he succeeded in affecting a landing, and clambering up the rocks he found himself in the presence of the dead chief, his family and relatives.

The cave smelt strongly of hot sulphurous vapors. With great care the mummies were removed, and all the little trinkets and ornaments scattered around were also taken away.

In all there are eleven packages of bodies. Only two or three have as yet been opened. The body of the chief is inclosed in a large basket-like structure, about four feet in height. Outside the wrappings are finely wrought sea-grass matting, exquisitely close in texture, and skins. At the bottom is a broad hoop or basket of thinly cut wood, and adjoining the center portions are pieces of body armor composed of reeds bound together. The body is covered with the fine skin of the sea-otter, always a mark of distinction in the interments of the Aleuts, and round the whole package are stretched the meshes of a fish-net, made of the sinews of the sea lion; also those of a bird-net. There are evidently some bulky articles inclosed with the chief's body, and the whole package differs very much from the others, which more resemble, in their brown-grass matting, consignments of crude sugar from the Sandwich Islands than the remains of human beings. The bodies of a pappoose and of a very little child, which probably died at birth or soon after it, have sea-otter skins around them. One of the feet of the latter projects, with a toe-nail visible. The remaining mummies are of adults.

One of the packages has been opened, and it reveals a man's body in tolerable preservation, but with a large portion of the face decomposed. This and the other bodies were doubled up at death by severing some of the muscles at the hip and knee joints and bending the limbs downward horizontally upon the trunk. Perhaps the most peculiar package, next to that of the chief, is one which incloses in a single matting, with sea-lion skins, the bodies of a man and woman. The collection also embraces a couple of skulls, male and female, which have still the hair attached to the scalp. The hair has changed its color to a brownish red. The relics obtained with the bodies include a few wooden vessels scooped out smoothly: a piece of dark, greenish, flat stone, harder than the emerald, which the Indians use to tan skins; a scalp-lock of jet-black hair; a small rude figure, which may have been a very ugly doll or an idol; two or three tiny carvings in ivory of

74

the sea-lion, very neatly executed; a comb, a necklet made of bird's claws inserted into one another, and several specimens of little bags, and a cap plaited out of sea-grass and almost water-tight.

In Cary's translation of Herodotus (1853, p. 180) the following passage occurs which purports to describe the manner in which the Macrobrian Ethiopians preserved their dead. It is added, simply as a matter of curious interest, nothing more, for no remains so preserved have ever been discovered.

After this, they visited last of all their sepulchres, which are said to be prepared from crystal in the following manner. When they have dried the body, either as the Egyptians do, or in some other way, they plaster it all over with gypsum, and paint it, making it as much as possible resemble real life; they then put round it a hollow column made of crystal, which they dig up in abundance, and is easily wrought. The body being in the middle of the column is plainly seen, nor does it emit an unpleasant smell, nor is it in any way offensive, and it is all visible as the body itself. The nearest relations keep the column in their houses for a year, offering to it the first-fruits of all, and performing sacrifices; after that time they carry it out and place it somewhere near the city.

Note.—The Egyptian mummies could only be seen in front, the back being covered by a box or coffin; the Ethiopian bodies could be seen all round, as the column of glass was transparent.

With the foregoing examples as illustration, the matter of embalmment may be for the present dismissed, with the advice to observers that particular care should be taken, in case mummies are discovered, to ascertain whether the bodies have been submitted to a regular preservative process, or owe their protection to ingredients in the soil of their graves or to desiccation in arid districts.

URN-BURIAL.

To close the subject of subterranean burial proper, the following account of urn-burial in Foster [37] may be added:

Urn-burial appears to have been practiced to some extent by the mound-builders, particularly in some of the Southern States. In the mounds on the Wateree River, near Camden, S.C., according to Dr. Blanding, ranges of vases, one above the other, filled with human remains, were found. Sometimes when the mouth of the vase is small the skull is placed with the face downward in the opening, constituting a sort of cover. Entire cemeteries have been found in which urn-burial alone seems to have been practiced. Such a one was accidentally discovered not many years since in Saint Catherine's Island, off the coast of Georgia. Professor Swallow informs me that from a mound at New Madrid, Mo., he obtained a human skull inclosed in an earthen jar, the lips of which were too small to admit of its extraction. It must therefore have been molded on the head after death.

A similar mode of burial was practiced by the Chaldeans, where the funeral jars often contain a human cranium much too expanded to admit of the possibility of its passing out of it, so that either the clay must have been modeled over the corpse, and then baked, or the neck of the jar must have been added subsequently to the other rites of interment. [38]

It is with regret that the writer feels obliged to differ from the distinguished author of the work quoted regarding urn-burial, for notwithstanding that it has been employed by some of the Central and Southern American tribes, it is not believed to have been customary, but *to a very limited extent*, in North America, except as a secondary interment. He must admit that he himself has found bones in urns or ollas in the graves of New Mexico and California, but under circumstances that would seem to indicate a deposition long subsequent to death. In the graves of the ancient peoples of California a number of ollas were found in long used burying places, and it is probable that as the bones were dug up time and again for new burials they were simply tossed into pots, which were convenient receptacles, or it may have been that bodies were allowed to repose in the earth long enough for the fleshy parts to decay, and the bones were then collected, placed in urns, and reinterred. Dr. E. Foreman, of the Smithsonian Institution, furnishes the following account of urns used for burial:

I would call your attention to an earthenware burial-urn and cover, Nos. 27976 and 27977, National Museum, but very recently received from Mr. William McKinley, of Milledgeville, Ga. It was exhumed on his plantation, ten miles below that city, on the bottom lands of the Oconee River, now covered with almost impassible canebrakes, tall grasses, and briers. We had a few months ago from the same source one of the covers, of which the ornamentation was different but more entire. A portion of a similar cover has been received also from Chattanooga, Tenn. Mr. McKinley ascribes the use of these urns and covers to the Muscogees, a branch of the Creek Nation.

These urns are made of baked clay, and are shaped somewhat like the ordinary steatite ollas found in the California coast graves, but the bottoms instead of being round run down to a sharp apex; on the top was a cover, the upper part of which also terminated in an apex, and around the border, near where it rested on the edge of the vessel, are indented scroll ornamentations.

The burial urns of New Mexico are thus described by E. A. Barber: [39]

Burial-urns   *   *   *   comprise vessels or ollas without handles, for cremation, usually being from 10 to 15 inches in height, with broad, open mouths, and made of coarse clay, with a laminated exterior (partially or entirely ornamented). Frequently the indentations extend simply around the neck or rim, the lower portion being plain.

So far as is known, up to the present time no burial-urns have been found in North America resembling those discovered in Nicaragua by Dr. J. C. Bransford, U.S.N., but it is quite within the range of possibility that future researches in regions not far distant from that which he explored may reveal similar treasures. Figure 6 represents different forms of burial-urns, *a*, *b*, and *e*, after Foster, are from Laporte, Ind. *f*, after Foster, is from Greenup County, Kentucky; *d* is from Milledgeville, Ga., in Smithsonian collection, No. 27976; and *c* is one of the peculiar shoe-shaped urns brought from Ometepec Island, Lake Nicaragua, by Surgeon J. C. Bransford, U.S.N.

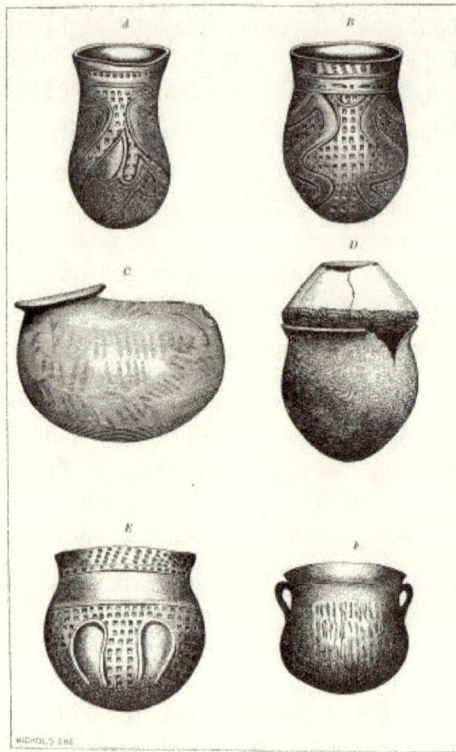

F$_{IG}$. 6.—Burial Urns.

SURFACE BURIAL.

This mode of interment was practiced to only a limited extent, so far as can be discovered, and it is quite probable that in most cases it was employed as a temporary expedient when the survivors were pressed for time. The Seminoles of Florida are said to have buried in hollow trees, the bodies being placed in an upright position, occasionally the dead being crammed into a hollow log lying on the ground. With some of the Eastern tribes a log was split in half and hollowed out sufficiently large to contain the corpse; it was then lashed together with withes and permitted to remain where it was originally placed. In some cases a pen was built over and around it. This statement is corroborated by R. S. Robertson, of Fort Wayne, Ind., who states, in a communication received in 1877, that the Miamis practiced surface burial in two different ways:

      *   *   *   1st. The surface burial in hollow logs. These have been found in heavy forests. Sometimes a tree has been split and the two halves hollowed out to receive the body, when it was either closed with withes or confined to the ground with crossed stakes; and sometimes a hollow tree is used by closing the ends.

2d. Surface burial where the body was covered by a small pen of logs laid up as we build a cabin, but drawing in every course until they meet in a single log at the top.

The writer has recently received from Prof. C. Engelhardt, of Copenhagen, Denmark, a brochure describing the oak coffins of Borum-Æshœi. From an engraving in this volume it would appear that the manner employed by the ancient Danes of hollowing out logs for coffins has its analogy among the North American Indians.

Romantically conceived, and carried out to the fullest possible extent in accordance with the *ante mortem* wishes of the dead, were the obsequies of Blackbird, the great chief of the Omahas. The account is given by George Catlin: [40]

He requested them to take his body down the river to this his favorite haunt, and on the pinnacle of this towering bluff to bury him on the back of his favorite war-horse, which was to be buried alive under him, from whence he could see, as he said, "the Frenchmen passing up and down the river in their boats." He owned, amongst many horses, a noble white steed, that was led to the top of the grass-covered hill, and with great pomp and ceremony, in the presence of the whole nation and several of the fur-traders and the Indian agent, he was placed astride of his horse's back, with his bow in his hand, and his shield and quiver slung, with his pipe and his medicine bag, with his supply of dried meat, and his tobacco-pouch replenished to last him through the journey to the beautiful hunting grounds of the shades of his fathers, with his flint, his steel, and his tinder to light his pipe by the way; the scalps he had taken from his enemies' heads could be trophies for nobody else, and were hung to the bridle of his horse. He was in full dress, and fully equipped, and on his head waved to the last moment his beautiful head-dress of the war-eagles' plumes. In this plight, and the last funeral honors having been performed by the medicine-men, every warrior of his band painted the palm and fingers of his right hand with vermillion, which was stamped and perfectly impressed on the milk-white sides of his devoted horse. This all done, turfs were brought and placed around the feet and legs of the horse, and gradually laid up to its sides, and at last over the back and head of the unsuspecting animal, and last of all over the head and even the eagle plumes of its valiant rider, where all together have smouldered and remained undisturbed to the present day.

Figure 7, after Schoolcraft, represents an Indian burial-ground on a high bluff of the Missouri River.

F_{IG}. 7.—Indian Cemetery.

According to the Rev. J. G. Wood, [41] the Obongo, an African tribe, buried their dead in a manner similar to that which has been stated of the Seminoles:

> When an Obongo dies it is usual to take the body to a hollow tree in the forest and drop it into the hollow, which is afterwards filled to the top with earth, leaves, and branches.

M. de la Potherie [42] gives an account of surface burial as practiced by the Iroquois of New York:

> Quand ce malade est mort, on le met sur son séant, on oint ses cheveux et tout son corps d'huile d'animaux, on lui applique du vermillon sur le visage; on lui met toutes sortes de beaux plumages de la rassade de la porcelaine et on le pare des plus beaux habits que l'on peut trouver, pendant que les parens et des vieilles continuent toujours à pleurer. Cette cérémonie finie, les alliez apportent plusieurs présens. Les uns sont pour essuyer les larmes et les autres pour servir de

80

matelas au défunt, on en destine certains pour couvrir la fosse, de peur, disent-ils, que la plague ne l'incommode, on y étend fort proprement des peaux d'ours et de chevreuils qui lui servent de lit, et on lui met ses ajustemens avec un sac de farine de bled d'Inde, de la viande, sa cuillière, et généralement tout ce qu'il faut à un homme qui veut faire un long voyage, avec toux les présens qui lui ont été faits á sa mort, et s'il a été guerrier on lui donne ses armes pour s'en servir au pais des morts. L'on couvre ensuite ce cadavre d'écorce d'arbres sur lesquelles on jette de la terre et quantité de pierres, et on l'entoure de pierres pour empêcher que les animaux ne le déterrent. Ces sortes de funérailles ne se font que dans leur village. Lorsqu'ils meurent en campagne on les met dans un cercueil d'écorce, entre les branches des arbres où on les élève sur quatre pilliers.

On observe ces mêmes funérailles aux femmes et aux filles. Tous ceux qui ont assisté aux obsèques profitent de toute la dépouille du défunt et s'il n'avoit rien, les parens y supléent. Ainsi ils ne pleurent pas en vain. Le deuil consiste à ne se point couper ni graisser les cheveux et de se tenir négligé sans aucune parure, couverts de méchantes hardes. Le père et la mère portent le deuil de leur fils. Si le père meurt les garçons le portent, et les filles de leur mère.

Dr. P. Gregg, of Rock Island, Illinois, has been kind enough to forward to the writer an interesting work by J. V. Spencer, [43] containing annotations by himself. He gives the following account of surface and partial surface burial occurring among the Sacs and Foxes formerly inhabiting Illinois:

Black Hawk was placed upon the ground in a sitting posture, his hands grasping his cane. They usually made a shallow hole in the ground, setting the body in up to the waist, so the most of the body was above ground. The part above ground was then covered by a buffalo robe, and a trench about eight feet square was then dug about the grave. In this trench they set picketing about eight feet high, which secured the grave against wild animals. When I first came here there were quite a number of these high picketings still standing where their chiefs had been buried, and the body of a chief was disposed of in this way while I lived near their village. The common mode of burial was to dig a shallow grave, wrap the body in a blanket, place it in the grave, and fill it nearly full of dirt; then take split sticks about three feet long and stand them in the grave so that their tops would come together in the form of a roof; then they filled in more earth so as to hold the sticks in place. I saw a father and mother start out alone to bury their child about a year old; they carried it by tieing it up in a blanket and putting a long stick through the blanket, each taking an end of the stick.

I have also seen the dead bodies placed in trees. This is done by digging a trough out of a log, placing the body in it, and covering it. I have seen several bodies in one tree. I think when they are disposed of in this way it is by special request, as I knew of an Indian woman who lived with a white family who desired her body placed in a tree, which was accordingly done. [44*] Doubtless there was some peculiar superstition attached to this mode, though I do not remember to have heard what it was.

Judge H. Welch [45] states that "the Sauks, Foxes, and Pottawatomies buried by setting the body on the ground and building a pen around it of sticks or logs. I think the bodies lay heads to the east." And C. C. Baldwin, of Cleveland, Ohio, sends a more detailed account, as follows:

I was some time since in Seneca County and there met Judge Welch.
 *   *   *   In 1824 he went with his father-in-law, Judge Gibson, to Fort Wayne. On the way they passed the grave of an Ottawa or Pottawatomie chief. The body lay on the ground covered with notched poles. It had been there but a few days and the worms were crawling around the body. My special interest in the case was the accusation of witchcraft against a young squaw who was executed for killing him by her arts. In the Summit County mounds there were only parts of skeletons with charcoal and ashes, showing they had been burned.

W. A. Brice [46] mentions a curious variety of surface burial not heretofore met with:

And often had been seen, years ago, swinging from the bough of a tree, or in a hammock stretched between two trees, the infant of the Indian mother; or a few little log inclosures, where the bodies of adults sat upright, with all their former apparel wrapped about them, and their trinkets, tomahawks, &c., by their side, could be seen at any time for many years by the few pale-faces visiting or sojourning here.

A method of interment so closely allied to surface burial that it may be considered under that head is the one employed by some of the Ojibways and Swampy Crees of Canada. A small cavity is scooped out, the body deposited therein, covered with a little dirt, the mound thus formed being covered either with split planks, poles, or birch bark.

Prof. Henry Youle Hind, who was in charge of the Canadian Red River exploring expedition of 1858, has been good enough to forward to the Bureau of Ethnology two photographs representing the variety of grave, which he found 15 or 20 miles from the present town of Winnipeg, and they are represented in the woodcuts, Figures 8 and 9.

F$_{\text{IG}}$. 8.—Grave Pen.

F$_{\text{IG}}$. 9.—Grave Pen.

CAIRN-BURIAL.

The next mode of interment to be considered is that of cairn or rock burial, which has prevailed and is still common to a considerable extent among the tribes living in the Rocky Mountains and the Sierra Nevadas.

In the summer of 1872 the writer visited one of these rock cemeteries in Middle Utah, which had been used for a period not exceeding fifteen or twenty years. It was situated at the bottom of a rock slide, upon the side of an almost inaccessible mountain, in a position so carefully chosen for concealment that it would have been almost impossible to find it without a guide. Several of the graves were opened, and found to have been constructed in the following manner: A number of bowlders had been removed from the bed of the slide until a sufficient cavity had been obtained; this was lined with skins, the corpse placed therein, with weapons, ornaments, &c., and covered over with saplings of the mountain aspen; on the top of these the removed bowlders were piled, forming a huge cairn, which appeared large enough to have marked the last resting place of an elephant. In the immediate vicinity of the graves were scattered the osseous remains of a number of horses which had been sacrificed, no doubt, during the funeral ceremonies. In one of the graves, said to contain the body of a chief, in addition to a number of articles useful and ornamental, were found parts of the skeleton of a boy, and tradition states that a captive boy was buried alive at this place.

From Dr. O. G. Given, physician to the Kiowa and Comanche Agency, Indian Territory, the following description of burial ceremonies was received. According to this gentleman the Kiowas call themselves *Kaw-a-wāh*, the Comanches *Nerm*, and the Apaches *Tāh-zee*.

> They bury in the ground or in crevices of rocks. They do not seem to have any particular rule with regard to the position. Sometimes prone, sometimes supine, but always decumbent. They select a place where the grave is easily prepared, which they do with such implements as they chance to have, viz, a squaw-axe, or hoe. If they are traveling, the grave is often very hastily prepared and not much time is spent in finishing. I was present at the burial of Black Hawk, an Apache chief, some two years ago, and took the body in my light wagon up the side of a mountain to the place of burial. They found a crevice in the rocks about four feet wide and three feet deep. By filling in loose rocks at either end they made a very nice tomb. The body was then put in face downwards, short sticks were put across, resting on projectionsof

84

rock at the sides, brush was thrown on this, and flat rocks laid over the whole of it.

The body of the deceased is dressed in the best clothing, together with all the ornaments most admired by the person when living. The face is painted with any colored paint they may have, mostly red and yellow, as I have observed. The body is then wrapped in skins, blankets, or domestic, with the hands laid across the breast, and the legs placed upon the thighs. They put into the grave their guns, bows and arrows, tobacco, and if they have it a blanket, moccasins, and trinkets of various kinds. One or more horses are killed over or near the grave. Two horses and a mule were killed near Black Hawk's grave. They were led up near and shot in the head. At the death of a Comanche chief, some years ago, I am told about seventy horses were killed, and a greater number than that were said to have been killed at the death of a prominent Kiowa chief a few years since.

The mourning is principally done by the relatives and immediate friends, although any one of their own tribe, or one of another tribe, who chances to be passing, will stop and moan with the relatives. Their mourning consists in a weird wail, which to be described must be heard, and once heard is never forgotten, together with the scarifying of their faces, arms, and legs with some sharp instrument, the cutting off of the hair, and oftentimes the cutting off of a joint of a finger, usually the little finger (Comanches do not cut off fingers). The length of time and intensity of their mourning depends upon the relation and position of the deceased in the tribe. I have known instances where, if they should be passing along where any of their friends had died, even a year after their death, they would mourn.

The Shoshones, of Nevada, generally concealed their dead beneath heaps of rocks, according to H. Butterfield, of Tyho, Nye County, Nevada, although occasionally they either burn or bury them. He gives as reasons for rock burial: 1st, to prevent coyotes eating the corpses; 2d, because they have no tools for deep excavations; and 3d, natural indolence of the Indians— indisposition to work any more than can be helped.

The Pi-Utes, of Oregon, bury in cairns; the Blackfeet do the same, as did also the Acaxers and Yaquis, of Mexico, and the Esquimaux; in fact, a number of examples might be quoted. In foreign lands the custom prevailed among certain African tribes, and it is said that the ancient Balearic Islanders covered their dead with a heap of stones, but this ceremony was preceded by an operation which consisted in cutting the body in small pieces and collecting in a pot.

CREMATION.

Next should be noted this mode of disposing of the dead, a common custom to a considerable extent among North American tribes, especially those living on the western slope of the Rocky Mountains, although we have undoubted evidence that it was also practiced, among the more eastern ones. This rite may be considered as peculiarly interesting from its great antiquity, for Tegg [47] informs us that it reached as far back as the Theban war, in the account of which mention is made of the burning of Menœacus and Archemorus, who were contemporary with Jair, eighth judge of Israel. It was common in the interior of Asia, and among the ancient Greeks and Romans, and has also prevailed among the Hindoos up to the present time. In fact, it is now rapidly becoming a custom among civilized people.

While there is a certain degree of similarity between the performance of this rite among the people spoken of and the Indians of North America, yet, did space admit, a discussion might profitably be entered upon regarding the details of it among the ancients and the origin of the ceremony. As it is, simple narrations of cremation in the country, with discursive notes and an account of its origin among the Nishinams of California, by Stephen Powers, [48] seem to be all that is required at this time:

> The moon and the coyote wrought together in creating all things that exist. The moon was good, but the coyote was bad. In making men and women, the moon wished to so fashion their souls that when they died they should return to the earth after two or three days as he himself does when he dies. But the coyote was evil disposed and said this should not be; but that when men died their friends should burn their bodies and once a year make a great mourning for them and the coyote prevailed. So, presently when deer died, they burned his body, as the coyote had decreed and after a year they made a great mourning for him. But the moon created the rattlesnake and caused it to bite the coyote's son, so that he died. Now, though the coyote had been willing to burn the deer's relations, he refused to burn his own son. Then the moon said unto him, "This is your own rule. You would have it so,

and now your son shall be burned like the others." So he was burned, and after a year the coyote mourned for him. Thus the law was established over the coyote also, and, as he had dominion over men, it prevailed over men likewise.

This story is utterly worthless for itself, but it has its value in that it shows there was a time when the California Indians did not practice cremation, which is also established by other traditions. It hints at the additional fact that the Nishinams to this day set great store by the moon, consider it their benefactor in a hundred ways and observe its changes for a hundred purposes.

Another myth regarding cremation is given by Adam Johnston in Schoolcraft [49] and relates to the Bonaks, or root-diggers:

The first Indians that lived were coyotes. When one of their number died the body became full of little animals or spirits, as they thought then. After crawling over the body for a time they took all manner of shapes, some that of the deer, others the elk, antelope, etc. It was discovered however, that great numbers were taking wings and for a while they sailed about in the air, but eventually they would fly off to the moon. The old coyotes or Indians, fearing the earth might become depopulated in this way, concluded to stop it at once and ordered that when one of their people died the body must be burnt. Ever after they continued to burn the bodies of deceased persons.

Ross Cox gives an account of the process as performed by the Tolkotins of Oregon: [50]

The ceremonies attending the dead are very singular and quite peculiar to this tribe. The body of the deceased is kept nine days laid out in his lodge and on the tenth it is buried. For this purpose a rising ground is selected, on which are laid a number of sticks, about 7 feet long, of cypress, neatly split and in the interstices, placed a quantity of gummy wood. During these operations invitations are dispatched to the natives of the neighboring villages requesting their attendance at the ceremony. When the preparations are perfected, the corpse is placed on the pile, which is immediately ignited and during the process of burning, the bystanders appear to be in a high state of merriment. If a stranger happen to be present they invariably plunder him, but if that pleasure be denied them, they never separate without quarreling among themselves. Whatever property the deceased possessed is placed about the corpse, and if he happened to be a person of consequence, his friends generally purchase a capote, a shirt, a pair of trousers, &c, which articles are also laid around the pile. If the doctor who attended him has escaped uninjured, he is obliged to be present at the ceremony, and for the last time tries his skill in restoring the defunct to animation. Failing in this, he throws on the body a piece of leather, or some other article, as a present, which in some measure appeases the resentment of his relatives, and preserves the unfortunate quack from being maltreated. During the nine days the corpse is laid out, the widow of the deceased is obliged to sleep along side it from sunset to sunrise, and from this custom there is no relaxation even during the hottest days of summer! While the doctor is performing his last operations she must lie on the pile, and after the fire is applied to it she cannot stir until the doctor orders her to be removed, which, however, is never done until her body is completely covered with blisters. After being placed on her legs, she is obliged to pass her hands gently through the flame and collect some of the liquid fat which issues from the corpse, with which she is permitted to wet her face and body. When the friends of the deceased observe the sinews of the legs and arms beginning to contract they compel the unfortunate widow to go again on the pile, and by dint of hard pressing to straighten those members.

If during her husband's life time she has been known to have committed any act of infidelity or omitted administering to him savory food or neglected his clothing, &c. she is now made to suffer severely for such lapses of duty by his relations, who frequently fling her in the funeral pile, from which she is dragged by her friends, and thus between alternate scorching and cooling she is dragged backwards and forwards until she falls into a state of insensibility.

After the process of burning the corpse has terminated, the widow collects the larger bones, which she rolls up in an envelope of birch bark and which she is obliged for some years afterwards to carry on her back. She is now considered and treated as a slave, all the laborious duties of cooking, collecting food, &c. devolve on her. She must obey the orders of all the women, and even of the children belonging to the village, and the slightest mistake or disobedience subjects her to the infliction of a heavy punishment. The ashes of her husband are carefully collected and deposited in a grave which it is her duty to keep free from weeds, and should any such appear, she is obliged to root them out with her fingers. During this operation her husband's relatives stand by and beat her in a cruel manner until the task is completed or she falls a victim to their brutality. The wretched widows, to avoid this complicated cruelty, frequently commit suicide. Should she, however, linger on for three or four years, the friends of her husband agree to relieve her from the her painful mourning. This is a ceremony of much consequence and the preparations for it occupy a considerable time generally from six to eight months. The hunters proceed to the various districts in which deer and beaver abound and after collecting large quantities of meat and fur return to the village. The skins are immediately bartered for guns, ammunition, clothing, trinkets, &c. Invitations are then sent to the inhabitants of the various friendly villages, and when they have all assembled the feast commences, and presents are distributed to each visitor. The object of their meeting is then explained, and the woman is brought forward, still carrying on her back the bones of her late husband, which are now removed and placed in a covered box, which is nailed or otherwise fastened to a post twelve feet high. Her conduct as a faithful widow is next highly eulogized, and the ceremony of her manumission is completed by one man powdering on her head the down of birds and another pouring on it the contents of a bladder of oil. She is then at liberty to marry again or lead a life of single blessedness, but few of them, I believe, wish to encounter the risk attending a second widowhood.

The men are condemned to a similar ordeal, but they do not bear it with equal fortitude, and numbers fly to distant quarters to avoid the brutal treatment which custom has established as a kind of religious rite.

Figure 10 is an ideal sketch of the cremation according to the description given.

F$_{IG}$. 10.—Tolkotin cremation.

Perhaps a short review of some of the peculiar and salient points of this narrative may be permitted.

It is stated that the corpse is kept nine days after death—certainly a long period of time, when it is remembered that Indians as a rule endeavor to dispose of their dead as soon as possible. This may be accounted for on the supposition that it is to give the friends and relatives an opportunity of assembling, verifying the death, and of making proper preparations for the ceremony. With regard to the verification of the dead person, William Sheldon [51] gives an account of a similar custom which was common among the Caraibs of Jamaica, and which seems to throw some light upon the unusual retention of deceased persons by the tribe in question, although it most be admitted that this is mere hypothesis:

> They had some very extraordinary customs respecting deceased persons. When one of them died, it was necessary that all his relations should see him and examine the body in order to ascertain that he died a natural death. They acted so rigidly on this principle, that if one relative remained who had not seen the body all the others could not convince that one that the death was natural. In such a case the absent relative considered himself as bound in honor to consider all the other relatives as having been accessories to the death of the kinsman, and did not rest until he had killed one of them to revenge the death of the deceased. If a Caraib died in Martinico or Guadaloupe and but his relations lived in St. Vincents, it was necessary to summon them to see the body, and several months sometimes elapsed before it couldbe

finally interred. When a Caraib died he was immediately painted all over with *roucou*, and had his mustachios and the black streaks in his face made with a black paint, which was different from that used in their lifetime. A kind of grave was then dug in the *carbet* where he died, about 4 feet square and 6 or 7 feet deep. The body was let down in it, when sand was thrown in, which reached to the knees, and the body was placed in it in a sitting posture, resembling that in which they crouched round the fire or the table when alive, with the elbows on the knees and the palms of the hands against the cheeks. No part of the body touched the outside of the grave, which was covered with wood and mats until all the relations had examined it. When the customary examinations and inspections were ended the hole was filled, and the bodies afterwards remained undisturbed. The hair of the deceased was kept tied behind. In this way bodies have remained several months without any symptoms of decay or producing any disagreeable smell. The *roucou* not only preserved them from the sun, air, and insects during their lifetime, but probably had the same effect after death. The arms of the Caraibs were placed by them when they were covered over for inspection, and they were finally buried with them.

Again, we are told that during the burning the bystanders are very merry. This hilarity is similar to that shown by the Japanese at a funeral, who rejoice that the troubles and worries of the world are over for the fortunate dead. The plundering of strangers present, it may be remembered, also took place among the Indians of the Carolinas. As already mentioned on a preceding page, the cruel manner in which the widow is treated seems to be a modification of the Hindoo suttee, but, if the account be true, it would appear that death might be preferable to such torments.

It is interesting to note that in Corsica, as late as 1743, if a husband died, women threw themselves upon the widow and beat her severely. Brohier quaintly remarks that this custom obliged women to take good care of their husbands.

George Gibbs, in Schoolcraft, [52] states that among the Indians of Clear Lake, California, "the body is consumed upon a scaffold built over a hole, into which the ashes are thrown and covered."

According to Stephen Powers, [53] cremation was common among the Se-nél of California. He thus relates it.

The dead are mostly burned. Mr. Willard described to me a scene of incremation that he once witnessed, which was frightful for its exhibitions of fanatic frenzy and infatuation. The corpse was that of a wealthy chieftain, and as he lay upon the funeral pyre they placed in his month two gold twenties, and other smaller coins in his ears and hands, on his breast, &c. besides all his finery, his feather mantles, plumes, clothing, shell money, his fancy bows, painted arrows, &c. When the torch was applied they set up a mournful ululation, chanting and dancing about him, gradually working themselves into a wild and ecstatic raving, which seemed almost a demoniacal possession, leaping, howling, lacerating their flesh. Many seemed to lose all self-control. The younger English-speaking Indians generally lend themselves charily to such superstitious work, especially if American spectators are present, but even they were carried away by the old contagious frenzy of their race. One stripped off a broadcloth coat, quite new and fine, and ran frantically yelling and cast it upon the blazing pile. Another rushed up, and was about to throw on a pile of California blankets, when a white man, to test his sincerity, offend him $16 for them, jingling the bright coins before his eyes, but the savage (for such he had become again for the moment) otherwise so avaricious, hurled him away with a yell of execration and ran and threw his offering into the flames. Squaws, even more frenzied, wildly flung upon the pyre all they had in the world—their dearest ornaments, their gaudiest dresses, their strings of glittering shells. Screaming, wailing, tearing their hair, beating their breasts in their mad and insensate infatuation, some of them would have cast themselves bodily into the flaming ruins and perished with the chief had they not been restrained by their companions. Then the bright, swift flames, with their hot tongues, licked this "cold obstruction" into chemic change, and the once "delighted spirit" of the savage was borne up. * * *

It seems as if the savage shared in Shakspeare's shudder at the thought of rotting in the dismal grave, for it is the one passion of his superstition to think of the soul, of his departed friend set free and purified by the swift purging heat of the flames not dragged down to be clogged and bound in the mouldering body, but borne up in the soft, warm chariots of the smoke toward the beautiful sun, to bask in his warmth and light, and then to fly away to the Happy Western Land. What wonder if the Indian shrinks with unspeakable horror from the thought of *burying his friend's soul!*—of pressing and ramming down with pitiless clods that inner something which once took such delight in the sweet light of the sun! What wonder if it takes years to persuade him to do otherwise and follow our custom! What wonder if even then he does it with sad fears and misgivings! Why not let him keep his custom! In the gorgeous landscapes and balmy climate of California an Indian incremation is as natural to the savage as it is for him to love the beauty of the sun. Let the vile Esquimaux and the frozen Siberian bury their dead if they will; it matters little, the earth is the same above as below; or to them the bosom of the earth may seem even the better; but in California do not blame the savage if he recoils at the thought of going underground! This soft pale halo of the lilac hills—ah, let him console himself if he will with the belief that his lost friend enjoys it still! The narrator concluded by saying that they destroyed full $500 worth of property. "The blankets," said he with a fine Californian scorn of much absurd insensibility to such a good bargain, "the blankets that the American offered him $16 for were not worth half the money."

After death the Se-nél hold that bad Indians return into coyotes. Others fall off a bridge which all souls must traverse, or are hooked off by a raging bull at the further end, while the good escape across. Like the Yokaia and the Konkan, they believe it necessary to nourish the spirits of the departed for the space of a year. This is generally done by a squaw, who takes pinole in her blanket, repairs to the scene of the incremation, or to places hallowed by the memory of the dead, when she scatters it over the ground, meantime rocking her body violently to and fro in a dance and chanting the following chorous:

Hel-lel-li-ly,

Hel-lel-lo,

Hel-lel-lu.

This refrain is repeated over and over indefinitely, but the words have no meaning whatever.

Henry Gillman [54] has published an interesting account of the exploration of a mound near Waldo, Fla., in which he found abundant evidence that cremation had existed among the former Indian population. It is as follows:

In opening a burial-mound at Cade's Pond, a small body of water situated about two miles northeastward of Santa Fé Lake, Fla., the writer found two instances of cremation, in each of which the skull of the subject, which was unconsumed, was used as the depository of his ashes. The mound contained besides a large number of human burials, the bones being much decayed. With them were deposited a great number of vessels of pottery, many of which are painted in brilliant colors, chiefly red, yellow, and brown, and some of them ornamented with indented patterns, displaying not a little skill in the ceramic art, though they are reduced to fragments. The first of the skulls referred to was exhumed at a depth of 2½ feet. It rested on its apex (base uppermost), and was filled with fragments of half incinerated human bones, mingled with dark-colored dust, and the sand which invariably sifts into crania under such circumstances. Immediately beneath the skull lay the greater part of a human tibia, presenting the peculiar compression known as a platycnemism to the degree of affording a latitudinal index of .512; while beneath and surrounding it lay the fragments of a large number of human bones, probably constituting an entire individual. In the second instance of this peculiar mode in cremation, the cranium was discovered on nearly the opposite side of the mound, at a depth of 2 feet, and, like the former, resting on its apex. It was filled with a black mass—the residuum of burnt human bones mingled with sand. At three feet to the eastward lay the shaft of a flattened tibia, which presents the longitudinal index of .527. Both the skulls were free from all action of fire, and though subsequently crumbling to pieces on their removal, the writer had opportunity to observe their strong resemblance to the small, orthocephalic crania which he had exhumed from mounds in Michigan. The same resemblance was perceptible in the other cranium belonging to this mound. The small narrow, retreating frontal, prominent parietal protuberances, rather protuberant occipital, which was not in the least compressed, the well defined supraciliary ridges, and the superior border of the orbits, presenting a quadrilateral outline, were also particularly noticed. The lower facial bones, including the maxillaries, were wanting. On consulting such works as are accessible to him, the writer finds no mention of any similar relics having been discovered in mounds in Florida, or elsewhere. For further particulars reference may be had to a paper on the subject read before the Saint Louis meeting of the American Association, August, 1878.

The discoveries made by Mr. Gillman would seem to indicate that the people whose bones he excavated resorted to a process of partial cremation, some examples of which will be given on another page. The use of crania as receptacles is certainly remarkable, if not unique.

The fact is well-known to archæologists that whenever cremation was practiced by Indians it was customary as a rule to throw into the blazing pyre all sorts of articles supposed to be useful to the dead, but no instance is known of such a wholesale destruction of property as occurred when the Indians of Southern Utah burned their dead, for Dr. E. Foreman relates, in the American Naturalist for July, 1876, the account of the exploration of a mound in that Territory, which proves that at the death of a person not only were the remains destroyed by fire, but all articles of personal property, even the very habitation which had served as a home. After the process was completed, what remained unburned was covered with earth and a mound formed.

A. S. Tiffany [55] describes what he calls a cremation-furnace, discovered within seven miles of Davenport, Iowa.

>   *   *   *   Mound seven miles, below the city, a projecting point known as Eagle Point. The surface was of the usual black soil to the depth of from 6 to 8 inches. Next was found a burnt indurated clay, resembling in color and texture a medium-burned brick, and about 30 inches in depth. Immediately beneath this clay was a bed of charred human remains 6 to 18 inches thick. This rested upon the unchanged and undisturbed loam of the bluffs, which formed the floor of the pit. Imbedded in this floor of unburned clay were a few very much decomposed, but unburned, human bones. No implements of any kind were discovered. The furnace appears to have been constructed by excavating the pit and placing at the bottom of it the bodies or skeletons which had possibly been collected from scaffolds, and placing the fuel among and above the bodies, with a covering of poles or split timbers extending over and resting upon the earth, with the clay covering above, which latter we now find resting upon the charred remains. The ends of the timber covering, where they were protected by the earth above and below, were reduced to charcoal,

parallel pieces of which were found at right angles to the length of the mound. No charcoal was found among or near the remains, the combustion there having been complete. The porous and softer portions of the bones were reduced to pulverized bone-black. Mr. Stevens also examined the furnace. The mound had probably not been opened after the burning.

This account is doubtless true, but the inferences may be incorrect.

Many more accounts of cremation among different tribes might be given to show how prevalent was the custom, but the above are thought to be sufficiently distinctive to serve as examples.

PARTIAL CREMATION.

Allied somewhat to cremation is a peculiar mode of burial which is supposed to have taken place among the Cherokees, or some other tribe of North Carolina, and which is thus described by J. W. Foster: [56]

Up to 1819 the Cherokee held possession of this region, when, in pursuance of a treaty, they vacated a portion of the lands lying in the valley of the Little Tennessee River. In 1821 Mr. McDowell commenced farming. During the first season's operations the plowshare, in passing over a certain portion of a field, produced a hollow rumbling sound, and in exploring for the cause the first object met with was a shallow layer of charcoal, beneath which was a slab of burnt clay about 7 feet in length and 4 feet broad, which, in the attempt to remove, broke into several fragments. Nothing beneath this slab was found, but on examining its under side, to his great surprise there was the mould of a naked human figure. Three of these burned-clay sepulchers were thus raised and examined during the first year of his occupancy, since which time none have been found until recently. During the past season, (1878) the plow brought up another fragment of one of these moulds, revealing the impress of a plump human arm.

Col. C. W. Jenkes, the superintendent of the Corundum mines, which have recently been opened in that vicinity, advises me thus:

"We have Indians all about us, with traditions extending back for 500 years. In this time they have buried their dead under huge piles of stones. We have at one point the remains of 600 warriors under one pile, but a grave has just been opened of the following construction:

A pit was dug, into which the corpse was placed, face upward; then over it was moulded a covering of mortar, fitting the form and features. On this was built a hot fire, which formed an entire shield of pottery for the corpse. The breaking up of one such tomb gives a perfect cast of the form of the occupant."

Colonel Jenkes, fully impressed with the value of these archeological discoveries, detailed a man to superintend the exhumation, who proceeded to remove the earth from the mould, which he reached through a layer of charcoal, and then with a trowel excavated beneath it. The clay was not thoroughly baked, and no impression of the corpse was left, except of the forehead and that portion of the limbs between the ankles and the knees, and even these portions of the mould crumbled. The body had been placed east and west, the head toward the east. "I had hoped," continues Mr. McDowell, "that the cast in the clay would be as perfect as one I found 51 years ago, a fragment of which I presented to Colonel Jenkes, with the impression of a part of the arm on one side and on the other of the fingers, that had pressed down the soft clay upon the body interred beneath it." The mound-builders of the Ohio valley, as has been shown, often placed a layer of clay over the dead, but not in immediate contact, upon which they builded fires; and the evidence that cremation was often resorted to in their disposition are too abundant to be gainsaid.

This statement is corroborated by Mr. Wilcox: [57]

Mr. Wilcox also stated that when recently in North Carolina his attention was called to an unusual method of burial by an ancient race of Indians in that vicinity. In numerous instances burial places were discovered where the bodies had been placed with the face up and covered with a coating of plastic clay about an inch thick. A pile of wood was then placed on top and fired, which consumed the body and baked the clay, which retained the impression of the body. This was then lightly covered with earth.

It is thought no doubt can attach to the statements given, but the cases are remarkable as being the only instances of the kind met with in the extensive range of reading preparatory to a study of the subject of burial, although it must be observed that Bruhier states that the ancient Ethiopians covered the corpses of their dead with plaster (probably mud), but they did not burn these curious coffins.

Another method, embracing both burial and cremation, has been practiced by the Pitt River or Achomawi Indians of California, who

Bury the body in the ground in a standing position, the shoulders nearly even with the ground. The grave is prepared by digging a hole of sufficient depth and circumference to admit the body, the head being cut off. In the grave are placed the bows and arrows, bead-work, trappings, &c., belonging to the deceased; quantities of food, consisting of dried fish, roots, herbs, &c., were placed with the body also. The grave was then filled up, covering the headless body; then a bundle of fagots was brought and placed on the grave by the different members of the tribe, and on these fagots the head was placed, the pile fired, and the head consumed to ashes; after this was done the female relatives of the deceased, who had appeared as mourners with their faces blackened with a preparation resembling tar or paint, dipped their fingers in the ashes of the cremated head and made three marks on their right cheek. This constituted the mourning garb, the period of which lasted until this black substance wore off from the face. In addition to this mourning, the blood female relatives of the deceased (who, by the way, appeared to be a man of distinction) had their hair cropped short. I noticed while the head was burning that the old women of the tribe sat on the ground, forming a large circle, inside of which another circle of young girls were formed standing and swaying their bodies to and fro and singing a mournful ditty. This was the only burial of a male that I witnessed. The custom of burying females is very different, their bodies being wrapped or bundled up in skins and laid away in caves, with their valuables and in some cases food being placed with them in their mouths. Occasionally money is left to pay for food in the spirit land.

This account is furnished by Gen. Charles H. Tompkins, deputy quartermaster-general, United States Army, who witnessed the burial above related, and is the more interesting as it seems to be the only well-authenticated case on record, although E. A. Barber [58] has described what may possibly have been a case of cremation like the one above noted:

A very singular case of aboriginal burial was brought to my notice recently by Mr. William Klingbeil, of Philadelphia. On the New Jersey bank of the Delaware River, a short distance below Gloucester City, the skeleton of a man was found buried in a standing position, in a high, red, sandy-clay bluff overlooking the stream. A few inches below the surface the neck bones were found, and below these the remainder of the skeleton, with the exception of the bones of the hands and feet. The skull being wanting, it could not be determined whether the remains were those of an Indian or of a white man, but in either case the sepulture was peculiarly aboriginal. A careful exhumation and critical examination by Mr. Klingbeil disclosed the fact that around the lower extremities of the body had been placed a number of large stones, which revealed traces of fire, in conjunction with charred wood, and the bones of the feet had undoubtedly been consumed. This fact makes it appear reasonably certain that the subject had been executed, probably as a prisoner of war. A pit had been dug, in which he was placed erect, and a fire kindled around him. Then he had been buried alive, or, at least, if he did not survive the fiery ordeal, his body was imbedded in the earth, with the exception of his head, which was left protruding above the surface. As no trace of the cranium could be found, it seems probable that the head had either been burned or severed from the body and removed, or else left a prey to ravenous birds. The skeleton, which would have measured fully six feet in height, was undoubtedly that of a man.

Blacking the face, as is mentioned in the first account, is a custom known to have existed among many tribes throughout the world, but in some cases different earths and pigments are used as signs of mourning. The natives of Guinea smear a chalky substance over their bodies as an outward expression of grief, and it is well known that the ancient Israelites threw ashes on their heads and garments. Placing food with the corpse or in its mouth, and money in the hand, finds its analogue in the custom of the ancient Romans, who, some time before interment, placed a piece of money in the corpse's mouth, which was thought to be Charon's fare for wafting the departed soul over the Infernal River. Besides this, the corpse's mouth was furnished with a certain cake, composed of flour, honey, &c. This was designed to appease the fury of Cerberus, the infernal doorkeeper, and to procure a safe and quiet entrance. These examples are curious coincidences, if nothing more.

AERIAL SEPULTURE.

LODGE-BURIAL.

Our attention should next be turned to sepulture above the ground, including lodge, house, box, scaffold, tree, and canoe burial, and the first example which may be given is that of burial in lodges, which is by no means common. The description which follows is by Stansbury, [59] and relates to the Sioux:

> I put on my moccasins, and, displaying my wet shirt like a flag to the wind, we proceeded to the lodges which had attracted our curiosity. There were five of them pitched upon the open prairie, and in them we found the bodies of nine Sioux laid out upon the ground, wrapped in their robes of buffalo-skin, with their saddles, spears, camp-kettles, and all their accoutrements piled up around them. Some lodges contained three, others only one body, all of which were more or less in a state of decomposition. A short distance apart from these was one lodge which, though small, seemed of rather superior pretensions, and was evidently pitched with great care. It contained the body of a young Indian girl of sixteen or eighteen years, with a countenance presenting quite an agreeable expression: she was richly dressed in leggins of fine scarlet cloth elaborately ornamented; a new pair of moccasins, beautifully embroidered with porcupine quills, was on her feet, and her body was wrapped in two superb buffalo-robes worked in like manner; she had evidently been dead but a day or two, and to our surprise a portion of the upper part of her person was bare, exposing the face and a part of the breast, as if the robes in which she was wrapped had by some means been disarranged, whereas all the other bodies were closely covered up. It was, at the time, the opinion of our mountaineers, that these Indians must have fallen in an encounter with a party of Crows; but I subsequently learned that they had all died of the cholera, and that this young girl, being considered past recovery, had been arranged by her friends in the habiliments of the dead, inclosed in the lodge alive, and abandoned to her fate, so fearfully alarmed were the Indians by this to them novel and terrible disease.

It might, perhaps, be said that this form of burial was exceptional, and due to the dread of again using the lodges which had served as the homes of those afflicted with the cholera, but it is thought such was not the case, as the writer has notes of the same kind of burial among the same tribe and of others, notably the Crows, the body of one of their chiefs (Long Horse) being disposed of as follows:

> The lodge poles inclose an oblong circle some 18 by 22 feet at the base, converging to a point, at least 30 feet high, covered with buffalo-

hides dressed without hair except a part of the tail switch, which floats outside like, and mingled with human scalps. The different skins are neatly fitted and sewed together with sinew, and all painted in seven alternate horizontal stripes of brown and yellow, decorated with various lifelike war scenes. Over the small entrance is a large bright cross, the upright being a large stuffed white wolf-skin upon his war lance, and the cross-bar of bright scarlet flannel, containing the quiver of bow and arrows, which nearly all warriors still carry, even when armed with repeating rifles. As the cross is not a pagan but a Christian (which Long Horse was not either by profession or practice) emblem, it was probably placed there by the influence of some of his white friends. I entered, finding Long Horse buried Indian fashion, in full war dress, paint and feathers, in a rude coffin, upon a platform about breast high, decorated with weapons, scalps, and ornaments. A large opening and wind-flap at the top favored ventilation, and though he had lain there in an open coffin a full month, some of which was hot weather, there was but little effluvia; in fact, I have seldom found much in a burial-teepee, and when this mode of burial is thus performed it is less repulsive than natural to suppose.

This account is furnished by Col. P. W. Norris, superintendent of Yellowstone National Park, he having been an eye-witness of what he relates in 1876; and although the account has been questioned, it is admitted for the reason that this gentleman persists, after a reperusal of his article, that the facts are correct.

General Stewart Van Vliet, U.S.A., informs the writer that among the Sioux of Wyoming and Nebraska when a person of consequence dies a small scaffold is erected inside his lodge and the body wrapped in skins deposited therein. Different utensils and weapons are placed by his side, and in front a horse is slaughtered; the lodge is then closed up.

Dr. W. J. Hoffman writes as follows regarding the burial lodges of the Shoshones of Nevada:

The Shoshones of the upper portion of Nevada are not known to have at any time practiced cremation. In Independence Valley, under a deserted and demolished *wickeup* or "brush tent," I found the dried-up corpse of a boy, about twelve years of age. The body had been here for at least six weeks, according to information received, and presented a shriveled and hideous appearance. The dryness of the atmosphere prevented decomposition. The Indians in this region usually leave the body when life terminates, merely throwing over it such rubbish as may be at hand, or the remains of their primitive shelter tents, which are mostly composed of small branches, leaves, grass, &c.

The Shoshones living on Independence Creek and on the eastern banks of the Owyhee River, upper portion of Nevada, did not bury their dead at the time of my visit in 1871. Whenever the person died, his lodge (usually constructed of poles and branches of *Salix*) was demolished and placed in one confused mass over his remains, when the band removed a short distance. When the illness is not too great, or death sudden, the sick person is removed to a favorable place, some distance from their temporary camping ground, so as to avoid the necessity of their own removal. Coyotes, ravens, and other carnivores soon remove all the flesh so that there remains nothing but the bones, and even these are scattered by the wolves. The Indians at Tuscarora, Nevada, stated that when it was possible and that they should by chance meet the bony remains of any Shoshone, they would bury it, but in what manner I failed to discover as the were very reticent, and avoided giving any information regarding the dead. One corpse was found totally dried and shrivelled, owing to the dryness of the atmosphere in this region.

Capt. F. W. Beechey [60] describes a curious mode of burial among the Esquimaux on the west coast of Alaska, which appears to be somewhat similar to lodge burial. Figure 11, after his illustration, affords a good idea of these burial receptacles.

Near us there was a burying ground, which in addition to what we had already observed at Cape Espenburg furnished several examples of the manner in which this tribe of natives dispose of their dead. In some instances a platform was constructed of drift-wood raised about two feet and a quarter from the ground, upon which the body was placed, with its head to the westward and a double tent of drift-wood erected over it, the inner one with spars about seven feet long, and the outer one with some that were three times that length. They were placed close together, and at first no doubt sufficiently so to prevent the depredations of foxes and wolves, but they had yielded at last, and all the bodies, and even the hides that covered them, had suffered by these rapacious animals.

In these tents of the dead there were no coffins or planks, as at Cape Espenburg, the bodies were dressed in a frock made of eider duck skins, with one of deer skin over it, and were covered with a sea horse hide, such as the natives use for their *baidars*. Suspended to the poles, and on the ground near them, were several Esquimaux implements, consisting of wooden trays, paddles, and a tamborine, which, we were informed as well as signs could convey the meaning of the natives, were placed there for the use of the deceased, who, in the next world (pointing to the western sky) ate, drank, and sang songs. Having no interpreter, this was all the information I could obtain, but the custom of placing such instruments around the receptacles of the dead is not unusual, and in all probability the Esquimaux may believe that the soul has enjoyments in the next world similar to those which constitute their happiness in this.

The Blackfeet, Cheyennes, and Navajos also bury in lodges, and the Indians of Bellingham Bay, according to Dr. J. F. Hammond, U.S.A., place their dead in carved wooden sarcophagi, inclosing these with a rectangular tent of some white material. Some of the tribes of the northwest coast bury in houses similar to those shown in Figure 12.

F<small>IG</small>. 12.—Burial Houses.

Bancroft [61] states that certain of the Indians of Costa Rica, when a death occurred, deposited the body in a small hut constructed of plaited palm reeds. In this it is preserved for three years, food being supplied, and on each anniversary of the death it is redressed and attended to amid certain ceremonies. The writer has been recently informed that a similar custom prevailed in Demerara. No authentic accounts are known of analogous modes of burial among the peoples of the Old World, although quite frequently the dead were interred beneath the floors of their houses, a custom which has been followed by the Mosquito Indians of Central America and one or two of our own tribes.

BOX-BURIAL.

Under this head may be placed those examples furnished by certain tribes on the northwest coast who used as receptacles for the dead wonderfully carved, large wooden chests, these being supported upon a low platform or resting on the ground. In shape they resemble a small house with an angular roof, and each one has an opening through which food may be passed to the corpse.

Some of the tribes formerly living in New York used boxes much resembling those spoken of, and the Creeks, Choctaws, and Cherokees did the same.

Capt. J. H. Gageby, United States Army, furnishes the following relating to the Creeks in Indian Territory.

      *   *   *   are buried on the surface, in a box or a substitute made

of branches of trees, covered with small branches, leaves, and earth. I have seen several of their graves, which after a few weeks had become uncovered and the remains exposed to view. I saw in one Creek grave (a child's) a small sum of silver, in another (adult male) some implements of warfare, bow and arrows. They are all interred with the feet of the corpse to the east. In the mourning ceremonies of the Creeks the nearer relatives smeared their hair and faces with a composition made of grease and wood ashes, and would remain in that condition for several days, and probably a month.

Josiah Priest [62] gives an account of the burial repositories of a tribe of Pacific coast Indians living on the Talomeco River, Oregon. The writer believes it to be entirely unreliable and gives it place as an example of credulity shown by many writers and readers.

The corpses of the Caciques were so well embalmed that there was no bad smell, they were deposited in large wooden coffins, well constructed, and placed upon benches two feet from the ground. In smaller coffins, and in baskets, the Spaniards found the clothes of the deceased men and women, and so many pearls that they distributed them among the officers and soldiers by handsfulls.

In Bancroft [63] may be found the following account of the burial boxes of the Esquimaux.

The Eskimos do not as a rule bury their dead, but double the body up and place it on the side in a plank box which is elevated three or four feet from the ground and supported by four posts. The grave-box is often covered with painted figures of birds, fishes and animals. Sometimes it is wrapped in skins placed upon an elevated frame and covered with planks or trunks of trees so as to protect it from wild beasts. Upon the frame, or in the grave box are deposited the arms, clothing, and sometimes the domestic utensils of the deceased. Frequent mention is made by travelers of burial places where the bodies lie exposed with their heads placed towards the north.

Frederic Whymper [64] describes the burial boxes of the Kalosh of that Territory.

Their grave boxes or tombs are interesting. They contain only the ashes of the dead. These people invariably burn the deceased. On one of the boxes I saw a number of faces painted, long tresses of human hair depending therefrom. Each head represented a victim of the (happily) deceased one's ferocity. In his day he was doubtless more esteemed than if he had never harmed a fly. All their graves are much ornamented with carved and painted faces and other devices.

W. H. Dall, [65] well known as one of the most experienced and careful of American Ethnologic observers, describes the burial boxes of the Innuits of Unalaklik, Innuits of Yuka, and Ingaliks of Ulukuk as follows: Figs. 13 and 14 are after his illustrations in the volume noted.

Fig. 13.—Innuit Grave.

INNUIT OF UNALAKLIK.

The usual fashion is to place the body doubled up on its side in a box of plank hewed out of spruce logs and about four feet long. This is elevated several feet above the ground on four posts which project above the coffin or box. The sides are often painted with red chalk in figures of fur animals, birds, and fishes. According to the wealth of the dead man, a number of articles which belonged to him are attached to the coffin or strewed around it; some of them have kyaks, bows and arrows, hunting implements, snow-shoes, or even kettles, around the grave or fastened to it; and almost invariably the wooden dish, or "kantág," from which the deceased was accustomed to eat, is hung on one of the posts.

F_{IG}. 14.—Ingalik grave.

INNUIT OF YUKON.

The dead are enclosed above ground in a box in the manner previously described. The annexed sketch shows the form of the sarcophagus, which, in this case, is ornamented with snow-shoes, a reel for seal-lines, a fishing-rod, and a wooden dish or kantág. The latter is found with every grave, and usually one is placed in the box with the body. Sometimes a part of the property of the dead person is placed in the coffin or about it; occasionally the whole is thus disposed of. Generally the furs, possessions, and clothing (except such as has been worn) are divided among the nearer relatives of the dead, or remain in possession of his family if he has one; such clothing, household utensils, and weapons as the deceased had in daily use are almost invariably enclosed in his coffin. If there are many deaths about the same time, or an epidemic occurs, everything belonging to the dead is destroyed. The house in which a death occurs is always deserted and usually destroyed. In order to avoid this, it is not uncommon to take the sick person out of the house and put him in a tent to die.

A woman's coffin may be known by the kettles and other feminine utensils about it. There is no distinction between the sexes in method of burial. On the outside of the coffin, figures are usually drawn in red ochre. Figures of fur animals usually indicate that the dead person was a good trapper; if seal or deer skin, his proficiency as a hunter; representation of parkies that he was wealthy; the manner of his death is also occasionally indicated. For four days after a death the women in the village do no sewing; for five days the men do not cut wood with an axe. The relatives of the dead must not seek birds' eggs on the overhanging cliffs for a year, or their feet will slip from under them and they will be dashed to pieces. No mourning is worn or indicated, except by cutting the hair. Women sit and watch the body, chanting a mournful refrain until he is interred. They seldom suspect that others have brought the death about by shamánism, as the Indians almost invariably do.

At the end of a year from the death, a festival is given, presents are made to those who assisted in making the coffin, and the period of mourning is over. Their grief seldom seems deep but they indulge for a long time in wailing for the dead at intervals. I have seen several women who refused to take a second husband, and had remained single in spite of repeated offers for many years.

INGALIKS OF ULUKUK.

As we drew near, we heard a low, wailing chant, and Mikála, one of my men, informed me that it was women lamenting for the dead. On landing, I saw several Indians hewing out the box in which the dead are placed. * * * The body lay on its side on a deer skin, the heels were lashed to the small of the back, and the head bent forward on the chest so that his coffin needed to be only about four feet long.

TREE AND SCAFFOLD BURIAL.

We may now pass to what may be called aerial sepulture proper, the most common examples of which are tree and scaffold burial, quite extensively practiced even at the present time. From what can be learned the choice of this mode depends greatly on the facilities present, where timber abounds, trees being used, if absent, scaffolds being employed.

From William J. Cleveland, of the Spotted Tail Agency, Nebraska, has been received a most interesting account of the mortuary customs of the Brulé or Teton Sioux, who belong to the Lakotah alliance. They are called *Sicaugu*, in the Indian tongue *Seechaugas*, or the "burned thigh" people. The narrative is given in its entirety, not only on account of its careful attention to details, but from its known truthfulness of description. It relates to tree and scaffold burial.

F_{IG}. 15.—Dakota Scaffold Burial.

FUNERAL CEREMONIES AND MOURNING OBSERVANCES.

Though some few of this tribe now lay their dead in rude boxes, either burying them when implements for digging can be had, or, when they have no means of making a grave, placing them on top of the ground on some hill or other slight elevation, yet this is done in imitation of the whites, and their general custom, as a people, probably does not differ in any essential way from that of their forefathers for many generations in the past. In disposing of the dead, they wrap the body tightly in blankets or robes (sometimes both) wind it all over with thongs made of the hide of some animal and place it reclining on the back at full length, either in the branches of some tree or on a scaffold made for the purpose. These scaffolds are about eight feet high and made by planting four forked sticks firmly in the ground, one at each corner and then placing others across on top, so as to form a floor on which the body is securely fastened. Sometimes more than one body is placed on the same scaffold, though generally a separate one is made for each occasion. These Indians being in all things most superstitious, attach a kind of sacredness to these scaffolds and all the materials used or about the dead. This superstition is in itself sufficient to prevent any of their own people from disturbing the dead, and for one of another nation to in any wise meddle with them is considered an offense not too severely punished by death. The same feeling also prevents them from ever using old scaffolds or any of the wood which has been used about them, even for firewood, though the necessity may be very great, for fear some evil consequences will follow. It is also the custom, though not universally followed, when bodies have been for two years on the scaffolds to take them down and bury them under ground.

All the work about winding up the dead, building the scaffold, and placing the dead upon it is done by women only, who, after having finished their labor, return and bring the men, to show them where the body is placed, that they may be able to find it in future. Valuables of all kinds, such as weapons, ornaments, pipes, &c.—in short, whatever the deceased valued most highly while living, and locks of hair cut from the heads of the mourners at his death, are always bound up with the body. In case the dead was a man of importance, or if the family could afford it, even though he were not, one or several horses (generally, in the former case, those which the departed thought most of) are shot and placed under the scaffold. The idea in this is that the spirit of the horse will accompany and be of use to his spirit in the "happy hunting grounds," or, as these people express it, "the spirit land."

When an Indian dies, and in some cases even before death occurs, the friends and relatives assemble at the lodge and begin crying over the departed or departing one. This consists in uttering the most heartrending, almost hideous wails and lamentations, in which all join until exhausted. Then the mourning ceases for a time until some one starts it again, when all join in as before and keep it up until unable to cry longer. This is kept up until the body is removed. This crying is done almost wholly by women, who gather in large numbers on such occasions, and among them a few who are professional mourners. These are generally old women and go whenever a person is expected to die, to take the leading part in the lamentations, knowing that they will be well paid at the distribution of goods which follows. As soon as death takes place, the body is dressed by the women in the best garments and blankets obtainable, new ones if they can be afforded. The crowd gathered near continue wailing piteously, and from time to time cut locks of hair from their own heads with knives, and throw them on the dead body. Those who wish to show their grief most strongly, cut themselves in various places, generally in the legs and arms, with their knives or pieces of flint, more commonly the latter, causing the blood to flow freely over their persons. This custom is followed to a less degree by the men.

A body is seldom kept longer than one day as, besides the desire to get the dead out of sight, the fear that the disease which caused the death will communicate itself to others of the family causes them to hasten the disposition of it as soon as they are certain that death has actually taken place.

Until the body is laid away the mourners eat nothing. After that is done, connected with which there seems to be no particular ceremony, the few women who attend to it return to the lodge and a distribution is made among them and others, not only of the remaining property of the deceased, but of all the possessions, even to the lodge itself of the family to which he belonged. This custom in some cases has been carried so far as to leave the rest of the family not only absolutely destitute but actually naked. After continuing in this condition for a time, they gradually reach the common level again by receiving gifts from various sources.

The received custom requires of women, near relatives of the dead, a strict observance of the ten days following the death, as follows: They are to rise at a very early hour and work unusually hard all day, joining in no feast, dance, game, or other diversion, eat but little, and retire late, that they may be deprived of the usual amount of sleep as of food. During this they never paint themselves, but at various times go to the top of some hill and bewail the dead in loud cries and lamentations for hours together. After the ten days have expired they paint themselves again and engage in the usual amusements of the people as before. The men are expected to mourn and fast for one day and then go on the war-path against some other tribe, or on some long journey alone. If he prefers, he can mourn and fast for two or more days and remain at home. The custom of placing food at the scaffold also prevails to some extent. If but little is placed there it is understood to be for the spirit of the dead, and no one is allowed to touch it. If much is provided, it is done with the intention that those of the same sex and age as the deceased shall meet there and consume it. If the dead be a little girl, the young girls meet and eat what is provided; if it be a man, then men assemble for the same purpose. The relatives never mention the name of the dead.

F_{IG}. 16.—Offering Food to the Dead.

"KEEPING THE GHOST."

Still another custom, though at the present day by no means generally
followed, is still observed to some extent among them. This is called
wanagee yuhapee, or "keeping the ghost." A little of the hair from the
head of the deceased being preserved is bound up in calico and articles
of value until the roll is about two feet long and ten inches or more in
diameter, when it is placed in a case made of hide handsomely
ornamented with various designs in different colored paints. When the
family is poor, however, they may substitute for this case blue or
scarlet blanket or cloth. The roll is then swung lengthwise between
two supports made of sticks, placed thus × in front of a lodge which
has been set apart for the purpose. In this lodge are gathered presents
of all kinds, which are given out when a sufficient quantity is
obtained. It is often a year and sometimes several years before this

distribution is made. During all this time the roll containing the hair of the deceased is left undisturbed in front of the lodge. The gifts as they are brought in are piled in the back part of the lodge, and are not to be touched until given out. No one but men and boys are admitted to the lodge unless it be a wife of the deceased, who may go in if necessary very early in the morning. The men sit inside, as they choose, to smoke, eat, and converse. As they smoke they empty the ashes from their pipes in the center of the lodge, and they, too, are left undisturbed until after the distribution. When they eat, a portion is always placed first under the roll outside for the spirit of the deceased. No one is allowed to take this unless a large quantity is so placed, in which case it may be eaten by any persons actually in need of food, even though strangers to the dead. When the proper time comes the friends of the deceased and all to whom presents are to be given are called together to the lodge and the things are given out by the man in charge. Generally this is some near relative of the departed. The roll is now undone and small locks of the hair distributed with the other presents, which ends the ceremony.

Sometimes this "keeping the ghost" is done several times, and it is then looked upon as a repetition of the burial or putting away of the dead. During all the time before the distribution of the hair, the lodge, as well as the roll, is looked upon as in a manner sacred, but after that ceremony it becomes common again and may be used for any ordinary purpose. No relative or near friend of the dead wishes to retain anything in his possession that belonged to him while living, or to see, hear, or own anything which will remind him of the departed. Indeed, the leading idea in all their burial customs in the laying away with the dead their most valuable possessions, the giving to others what is left of his and the family property, the refusal to mention his name, &c., is to put out of mind as soon and as effectual as possible the memory of the departed.

From what has been said, however, it will be seen that they believe each person to have a spirit which continues to live after the death of the body. They have no idea of a future life in the body, but believe that after death their spirits will meet and recognize the spirits of their departed friends in the spirit land. They deem it essential to their happiness here, however, to destroy as far as practicable their recollection of the dead. They frequently speak of death as a sleep, and of the dead as asleep or having gone to sleep at such a time. These customs are gradually losing their hold upon them, and are much less generally and strictly observed than formerly.

Figure 15 furnishes a good example of scaffold burial. Figure 16, offering of food and drink to the dead. Figure 17, depositing the dead upon the scaffold.

F<small>IG</small>. 17.—Depositing the Corpse.

A. Delano, [66] mentions as follows an example of tree-burial which he noticed in Nebraska.

    *   *   *   During the afternoon we passed a Sioux burying-ground, if I may be allowed to use an Irishism. In a hackberry tree, elevated about twenty feet from the ground, a kind of rack was made of broken tent poles, and the body (for there was but one) was placed upon it, wrapped in his blanket, and a tanned buffalo skin, with his tin cup, moccasins, and various things which he had used in life, were placed upon his body, for his use in the land of spirits.

114

Figure 18 represents tree-burial, from a sketch drawn by my friend Dr. Washington Matthews, United States Army.

Fig. 18.—Tree-burial.

John Young, Indian agent at the Blackfeet Agency, Montana, sends the following account of tree-burial among this tribe:

> Their manner of burial has always been (until recently) to inclose the dead body in robes or blankets, the best owned by the departed, closely sewed up, and then, if a male or chief, fasten in the branches of a tree so high as to be beyond the reach of wolves, and then left to slowly waste in the dry winds. If the body was that of a squaw or child, it was thrown into the underbrush or jungle, where it soon became the prey of the wild animals. The weapons, pipes, &c., of men were inclosed, and the small toys of children with them. The ceremonies were equally barbarous, the relatives cutting off, according

to the depth of their grief, one or more joints of the fingers, divesting themselves of clothing even in the coldest weather, and filling the air with their lamentations. All the sewing up and burial process was conducted by the squaws, as the men would not touch nor remain in proximity to a dead body.

The following account of scaffold burial among the Gros Ventres and Mandans of Dakota is furnished by E. H. Alden, United States Indian agent at Fort Berthold:

> The Gros Ventres and Mandans never bury in the ground, but always on a scaffold, made of four posts about eight feet high, on which the box is placed, or, if no box is used, the body wrapped in red or blue cloth if able, or, if not, a blanket of cheapest white cloth, the tools and weapons being placed directly under the body, and there they remain forever, no Indian ever daring to touch one of them. It would be bad medicine to touch the dead or anything so placed belonging to him. Should the body by any means fall to the ground, it is never touched or replaced on the scaffold. As soon as one dies he is immediately buried, sometimes within an hour, and the friends begin howling and wailing as the process of interment goes on, and continue mourning day and night around the grave, without food sometimes three or four days. Those who mourn are always paid for it in some way by the other friends of the deceased, and those who mourn the longest are paid the most. They also show their grief and affection for the dead by a fearful cutting of their own bodies, sometimes only in part, and sometimes all over their whole flesh, and this sometimes continues for weeks. Their hair, which is worn in long braids, is also cut off to show their mourning. They seem proud of their mutilations. A young man who had just buried his mother came in boasting of, and showing his mangled legs.

According to Thomas L. McKenney, [67] the Chippewas of Fond du Lac, Wis., buried on scaffolds, inclosing the corpse in a box. The narrative is as follows:

> One mode of burying the dead among the Chippewas is to place the coffin or box containing their remains on two cross-pieces, nailed or tied with wattap to four poles. The poles are about ten feet high. They plant near these posts the wild hop or some other kind of running vine, which spreads over and covers the coffin. I saw one of these on the island, and as I have described it. It was the coffin of a child about four years old. It was near the lodge of the sick girl. I have a sketch of

it. I asked the chief why his people disposed of their dead in that way. He answered they did not like to put them out of their sight so soon by putting them under ground. Upon a platform they could see the box that contained their remains, and that was a comfort to them.

Figure 19 is copied from McKenney's picture of this form of burial.

Fɪɢ. 19.—Chippewa Scaffold Burial.

Keating [68] thus describes burial scaffolds:

On these scaffolds, which are from eight to ten feet high, corpses were deposited in a box made from part of a broken canoe. Some hair was suspended, which we at first mistook for a scalp, but our guide informed us that these were locks of hair torn from their heads by the relatives to testify their grief. In the center, between the four posts which supported the scaffold, a stake was planted in the ground, it was about six feet high, and bore an imitation of human figures, five of which had a design of a petticoat indicating them to be females; the rest amounting to seven, were naked and were intended for male figures; of the latter four were headless, showing that they had been slain, the three other male figures were unmutilated, but held a staff in their hand, which, as our guide informed us designated that they were slaves. The post, which is an usual accompaniment to the scaffold that supports a warrior's remains, does not represent the achievements of the deceased, but those of the warriors that assembled near his remains danced the dance of the post, and related their martial exploits.

A number of small bones of animals were observed in the vicinity, which were probably left there after a feast celebrated in honor of the dead.

The boxes in which the corpses were placed are so short that a man could not lie in them extended at full length, but in a country where boxes and boards are scarce this is overlooked. After the corpses have remained a certain time exposed, they are taken down and burned. Our guide, Renville, related to us that he had been a witness to an interesting, though painful, circumstance that occurred here. An Indian who resided on the Mississippi, hearing that his son had died at this spot, came up in a canoe to take charge of the remains and convey them down the river to his place of abode but on his arrival he found that the corpse had already made such progress toward decomposition as rendered it impossible for it to be removed. He then undertook with a few friends, to clean off the bones. All the flesh was scraped off and thrown into the stream, the bones were carefully collected into his canoe, and subsequently carried down to his residence.

Interesting and valuable from the extreme attention paid to details is the following account of a burial case discovered by Dr. George M. Sternberg, United States Army, and furnished by Dr. George A. Otis, United States Army, Army Medical Museum, Washington, D.C. It relates to the Cheyennes of Kansas.

The case was found, Brevet Major Sternberg states, on the banks of Walnut Creek, Kansas, elevated about eight feet from the ground by four notched poles, which were firmly planted in the ground. The unusual care manifested in the preparation of the case induced Dr. Sternberg to infer that some important chief was inclosed in it. Believing that articles of interest were inclosed with the body, and that their value would be enhanced if the were received at the Museum as left by the Indians, Dr. Sternberg determined to send the case unopened.

I had the case opened this morning and an inventory made of the contents. The case consisted of a cradle of interlaced branches of white willow, about six feet long, three feet broad, and three feet high, with a flooring of buffalo thongs arranged as a net-work. This cradle was securely fastened by strips of buffalo-hide to four poles of ironwood and cottonwood, about twelve feet in length. These poles doubtless rested upon the forked extremities of the vertical poles described by Dr. Sternberg. The cradle was wrapped in two buffalo robes of large size and well preserved. On removing these an aperture eighteen inches square was found at the middle of the right-side of the cradle or basket. Within appeared other buffalo robes folded about the remains, and secured by gaudy-colored sashes. Five robes were successively removed, making seven in all. Then we came to a series of new blankets folded about the remains. There were five in all—two scarlet, two blue, and one white. These being removed, the next wrappings consisted of a striped white and gray sack, and of a United States Infantry overcoat, like the other coverings nearly new. We had now come apparently upon the immediate envelope of the remains, which it was now evident must be those of a child. These consisted of three robes, with hoods very richly ornamented with bead-work. These robes or cloaks were of buffalo-calf skin about four feet in length, elaborately decorated with bead-work in stripes. The outer was covered with rows of blue and white bead-work, the second was green and yellow, and the third blue and red. All were further adorned by spherical brass bells attached all about the borders by strings of beads.

The remains with their wrappings lay upon a matting similar to that used by the Navajo and other Indians of the southern plains, and upon a pillow of dirty rags, in which were folded a bag of red paint, bits of antelope skin, bunches of straps, buckles, &c. The three bead-work hooded cloaks were now removed, and then we successively unwrapped a gray woolen double shawl, five yards of blue cassimere, six yards of red calico, and six yards of brown calico, and finally disclosed the remains of a child, probably about a year old, in an advanced stage of decomposition. The cadaver had a beaver-cap ornamented with disks of copper containing the bones of the cranium, which had fallen apart. About the neck were long wampum necklaces, with *Dentalium*, *Unionidæ*, and *Auriculæ*, interspersed with beads. There were also strings of the pieces of *Haliotis* from the Gulf of California, so valued by the Indians on this side of the Rocky Mountains. The body had been elaborately dressed for burial, the costume consisting of a red-flannel cloak, a red tunic, and frock-leggins adorned with bead-work, yarn stockings of red and black worsted, and deer-skin beadwork moccasins. With the remains were numerous trinkets, a porcelain image, a China vase, strings of beads, several toys, a pair of mittens, a fur collar, a pouch of the skin of *Putorius vison*, &c.

Another extremely interesting account of scaffold-burial, furnished by Dr. L. S. Turner, United States Army, Fort Peck, Mont., and relating to the Sioux, is here given entire, as it refers to certain curious mourning observances which have prevailed to a great extent over the entire globe:

The Dakotas bury their dead in the tops of trees when limbs can be found sufficiently horizontal to support scaffolding on which to lay the body, but as such growth is not common in Dakota, the more general practice is to lay them upon scaffolds from seven to ten feet high and out of the reach of carnivorous animals, as the wolf. These scaffolds are constructed upon four posts set into the ground something after the manner of the rude drawing which I inclose. Like all labors of a domestic kind, the preparation for burial is left to the women, usually the old women. The work begins as soon as life is extinct. The face, neck, and hands are thickly painted with vermilion, or a species of red earth found in various portions of the Territory when the vermilion of the traders cannot be had. The clothes and personal trinkets of the deceased ornament the body. When blankets are available, it is then wrapped in one, all parts of the body being completely enveloped. Around this a dressed skin of buffalo is then securely wrapped, with the flesh side out, and the whole securely bound with thongs of skins, either raw or dressed; and for ornament, when available, a bright-red blanket envelopes all other coverings, and renders the general scene more picturesque until dimmed by time and the elements. As soon as the scaffold is ready, the body is borne by the women, followed by the female relatives, to the place of final deposit, and left prone in its secure wrappings upon this airy bed of death. This ceremony is accompanied with lamentations wild and weird that one must see and hear in order to appreciate. If the deceased be a brave, it is customary to place upon or beneath the scaffold a few buffalo-heads which time has rendered dry and inoffensive; and if he has been brave in war some of his implements of battle are placed on the scaffold or securely tied to its timbers. If the deceased has been a chief, or a soldier related to his chief, it is not uncommon to slay his favorite pony and place the body beneath the scaffold, under the superstition, I suppose, that the horse goes with the man. As illustrating the propensity to provide the dead with the things used while living, I may mention that some years ago I loaned to an old man a delft urinal for the use of his son, a young man who was slowly dying of a wasting disease. I made him promise faithfully that he would return it as soon as his son was done using it. Not long afterwards the urinal graced the scaffold which held the remains of the dead warrior, and as it has not to this day been returned I presume the young man is not done using it.

The mourning customs of the Dakotas, though few of them appear to be of universal observance, cover considerable ground. The hair, never cut under other circumstances, is cropped off even with the neck, and the top of the head and forehead, and sometimes nearly the whole body, are smeared with a species of white earth resembling chalk, moistened with water. The lodge, teepee, and all the family possessions except the few shabby articles of apparel worn by the mourners, are given away and the family left destitute. Thus far the custom is universal or nearly so. The wives, mother, and sisters of a deceased man, on the first, second, or third day after the funeral, frequently throw off their moccasins and leggings and gash their legs with their butcher-knives, and march through the camp and to the place of burial with bare and bleeding extremities, while they chant or wail their dismal songs of mourning. The men likewise often gash themselves in many places, and usually seek the solitude of the higher point on the distant prairie, where they remain fasting, smoking, and wailing out their lamentations for two or three days. A chief who had lost a brother once came to me after three or four days of mourning in solitude almost exhausted from hunger and bodily anguish. He had gashed the outer side of both lower extremities at intervals of a few inches all the way from the ankles to the top of the hips. His wounds had inflamed from exposure, and were suppurating freely. He assured me that he had not slept for several days or nights. I dressed his wounds with a soothing ointment, and gave him a full dose of an effective anodyne, after which he slept long and refreshingly, and awoke to express his gratitude and shake my hand in a very cordial and sincere manner. When these harsher inflictions are not resorted to, the mourners usually repair daily for a few days to the place of burial, toward the hour of sunset, and chant their grief until it is apparently assuaged by its own expression. This is rarely kept up for more than four or five days, but is occasionally resorted to, at intervals, for weeks, or even months, according to the mood of the bereft. I have seen few things in life so touching as the spectacle of an old father going daily to the grave of his child, while the shadows are lengthening, and pouring out his grief in wails that would move a demon, until his figure melts with the gray twilight, when, silent and solemn, he returns to his desolate family. The weird effect of this observance is sometimes heightened, when the deceased was a grown-up son, by the old man kindling a little fire near the head of the scaffold, and varying his lamentations with smoking in silence. The foregoing is drawn from my memory of personal observances during a period of more than six years' constant intercourse with several subdivisions of the Dakota Indians. There may be much which memory has failed to recall upon a brief consideration.

Figure 20 represents scarification as a form of grief-expression for the dead.

Fig. 20.—Scarification at Burial.

Perhaps a brief review of Dr. Turner's narrative may not be deemed inappropriate here.

Supplying food to the dead is a custom which is known to be of great antiquity; in some instances, as among the ancient Romans, it appears to have been a sacrificial offering, for it usually accompanied cremation, and was not

122

confined to food alone, for spices, perfumes, oil, &c., were thrown upon the burning pile. In addition to this, articles supposed or known to have been agreeable to the deceased were also consumed. The Jews did the same, and in our own time the Chinese, Caribs, and many of the tribes of North American Indians followed these customs. The cutting of hair as a mourning observance is of very great antiquity, and Tegg relates that among the ancients whole cities and countries were shaved (*sic*) when a great man died. The Persians not only shaved themselves on such occasions, but extended the same process to their domestic animals, and Alexander, at the death of Hephæstin, not only cut off the manes of his horses and mules, but took down the battlements from the city walls, that even towns might seem in mourning and look bald. Scarifying and mutilating the body has prevailed from a remote period of time, having possibly replaced, in the process of evolution, to a certain extent, the more barbarous practice of absolute personal sacrifice. In later days, among our Indians, human sacrifices have taken place to only a limited extent, but formerly many victims were immolated, for at the funerals of the chiefs of the Florida and Carolina Indians all the male relatives and wives were slain, for the reason, according to Gallatin, that the hereditary dignity of Chief or Great Sun descended, as usual, by the female line, and he, as well as all other members of his clan, whether male or female, could marry only persons of an inferior clan. To this day mutilation of the person among some tribes of Indians is usual. The sacrifice of the favorite horse or horses is by no means peculiar to our Indians, for it was common among the Romans, and possibly even among the men of the Reindeer period, for at Solutré, in France, the writer saw horses' bones exhumed from the graves examined in 1873. The writer has frequently conversed with Indians upon this subject, and they have invariably informed him that when horses were slain great care was taken to select the poorest of the band.

Tree-burial was not uncommon among the nations of antiquity, for the Colchians enveloped their dead in sacks of skin and hung them to trees; the ancient Tartars and Scythians did the same. With regard to the use of scaffolds and trees as places of deposit for the dead, it seems somewhat curious that the tribes who formerly occupied the eastern portion of our continent were not in the habit of burying in this way, which, from the abundance of timber, would have been a much easier method than the ones in vogue, while the western tribes, living in sparsely-wooded localities, preferred the other. If we consider that the Indians were desirous of preserving their dead as long as possible, the fact of their dead being placed in trees and scaffolds would lead to the supposition that those living on the plains were well aware of the desiccating property of the dry air of that arid region. This desiccation would pass for a kind of mummification.

The particular part of the mourning ceremonies, which consisted in loud cries and lamentations, may have had in early periods of time a greater significance than that of a mere expression of grief or woe, and on this point Bruhier [69] seems quite positive, his interpretation being that such cries were intended to prevent premature burial. He gives some interesting examples, which may be admitted here:

> The Caribs lament loudly, their wailings being interspersed with comical remarks and questions to the dead as to why he preferred to leave this world, having everything to make life comfortable. They place the corpse on a little seat in a ditch or grave four or five feet deep, and for ten days they bring food, requesting the corpse to eat. Finally, being convinced that the dead will neither eat nor return to life, they throw the food on the head of the corpse and fill up the grave.

When one died among the Romans, the nearest relatives embraced the body, closed the eyes and month, and when one was about to die received the last words and sighs, and then loudly called the name of the dead, finally bidding an eternal adieu. This ceremony of calling the deceased by name was known as the *conclamation*, and was a custom anterior even to the foundation of Rome. One dying away from home was immediately removed thither, in order that this might be performed with greater propriety. In Picardy, as late as 1743, the relatives threw themselves on the corpse and with loud cries called it by name, and up to 1855 the Moravians of Pennsylvania, at the death of one of their number, performed mournful musical airs on brass instruments from the village church steeple and again at the grave [70*]. This custom, however, was probably a remnant of the ancient funeral observances, and not to prevent premature burial, or, perhaps, was intended to scare away bad spirits.

W. L. Hardisty [71] gives a curious example of log-burial in trees, relating to the Loucheux of British America:

> They inclose the body in a neatly-hollowed piece of wood, and secure it to two or more trees, about six feet from the ground. A log about eight feet long is first split in two, and each of the parts carefully hollowed out to the required size. The body is then inclosed and the two pieces well lashed together, preparatory to being finally secured, as before stated, to the trees.

The American Indians are by no means the only savages employing scaffolds as places of deposit for the dead, for Wood [72] gives a number of examples of this mode of burial.

F_{IG}. 21.—Australian Scaffold Burial.

In some parts of Australia the natives, instead of consuming the body by fire, or hiding it in caves or in graves, make it a peculiarly conspicuous object. Should a tree grow favorably for their purpose, they will employ it as the final resting place for the dead body. Lying in its canoe coffin, and so covered over with leaves and grass that its shape is quite disguised, the body is lifted into a convenient fork of the tree and lashed to the boughs, by native ropes. No farther care is taken of it, and if in process of time it should be blown out of the tree, no one will take the trouble of replacing it.

Should no tree be growing in the selected spot, an artificial platform is made for the body, by fixing the ends of stout branches in the ground and connecting them at their tops by smaller horizontal branches. Such are the curious tombs which are represented in the illustration.

* * * These strange tombs are mostly placed among the reeds, so that nothing can be more mournful than the sound of the wind as it shakes the reeds below the branch in which the corpse is lying. The object of this aerial tomb is evident enough, namely, to protect the corpse from the dingo, or native dog. That the ravens and other carrion-eating birds should make a banquet upon the body of the dead man does not seem to trouble the survivors in the least, and it often happens that the traveler is told by the croak of the disturbed ravens that the body of a dead Australian is lying in the branches over his head.

The aerial tombs are mostly erected for the bodies of old men who have died a natural death; but when a young warrior has fallen in battle the body is treated in a very different manner. A moderately high platform is erected, and upon this is seated the body of the dead warrior with the face toward the rising sun. The legs are crossed and the arms kept extended by means of sticks. The fat is then removed, and after being mixed with red ochre is rubbed over the body, which has previously been carefully denuded of hair, as is done in the ceremony of initiation. The legs and arms are covered with zebra-like stripes of red, white, and yellow, and the weapons of the dead man are laid across his lap.

The body being thus arranged, fires are lighted under the platform, and kept up for ten days or more, during the whole of which time the friends and mourners remain by the body, and are not permitted to speak. Sentinels relieve each other at appointed intervals, their duty being to see that the fires are not suffered to go out, and to keep the flies away by waving leafy boughs or bunches of emu feathers. When a body has been treated in this manner it becomes hard and mummy-like, and the strongest point is that the wild dogs will not touch it after it has been so long smoked. It remains sitting on the platform for two months or so, and is then taken down and buried, with the exception of the skull, which is made into a drinking-cup for the nearest relative.

* * *

This mode of mummifying resembles somewhat that already described as the process by which the Virginia kings were preserved from decomposition.

Figs. 21 and 22 represent the Australian burials described, and are after the

126

original engravings in Wood's work. The one representing scaffold-burial resembles greatly the scaffolds of our own Indians.

FIG. 22.—Preparing the Dead.

With regard to the use of scaffolds as places of deposit for the dead, the following theories by Dr. W. Gardner, United States Army, are given:

> If we come to inquire why the American aborigines placed the dead bodies of their relatives and friends in trees, or upon scaffolds resembling trees, instead of burying them in the ground, or burning them and preserving their ashes in urns, I think we can answer the inquiry by recollecting that most if not all the tribes of American Indians, as well as other nations of a higher civilization, believed that the human soul, spirit, or immortal part was of the form and nature of a bird, and as these are essentially arboreal in their habits, it is quite in keeping to suppose that the soul-bird would have readier access to its former home or dwelling-place if it was placed upon a tree or scaffold than if it was buried in the earth; moreover, from this lofty eyrie the souls of the dead could rest secure from the attacks of wolves or other profane beasts, and guard like sentinels the homes and hunting-grounds of their loved ones.

This statement is given because of a corroborative note in the writer's possession, but he is not prepared to admit it as correct without farther investigation.

PARTIAL SCAFFOLD BURIAL AND OSSUARIES.

Under this heading may be placed the burials which consisted in first depositing the bodies on scaffolds, where they were allowed to remain for a variable length of time, after which the bones were cleaned and deposited either in the earth or in special structures, called by writers "bone-houses." Roman [73] relates the following concerning the Choctaws:

The following treatment of the dead is very strange.   *   *   *   As soon as the deceased is departed, a stage is erected (as in the annexed plate is represented) and the corpse is laid on it and covered with a bear-skin; if he be a man of note, it is decorated, and the poles painted red with vermillion and bear's oil; if a child, it is put upon stakes set across; at this stage the relations come and weep, asking many questions of the corpse, such as, why he left them? did not his wife serve him well? was he not contented with his children? had he not corn enough? did not his land produce sufficient of everything? was he afraid of his enemies? &c., and this accompanied by loud howlings; the women will be there constantly, and sometimes, with the corrupted air and heat of the sun, faint so as to oblige the bystanders to carry them home; the men will also come and mourn in the same manner, but in the night or at other unseasonable times when they are least likely to be discovered.

The stage is fenced round with poles; it remains thus a certain time, but not a fixed space; this is sometimes extended to three or four months, but seldom more than half that time. A certain set of venerable old Gentlemen, who wear very long nails as a distinguishing badge on the thumb, fore, and middle finger of each hand, constantly travel through the nation (when I was there I was told there were but five of this respectable order) that one of them may acquaint those concerned, of the expiration of this period, which is according to their own fancy; the day being come, the friends and relations assemble near the stage, a fire is made, and the respectable operator, after the body is taken down, with his nails tears the remaining flesh off the bones, and throws it with the entrails into the fire, where it is consumed; then he scrapes the bones and burns the scrapings likewise; the head being painted red with vermillion is with the rest of the bones put into a neatly made chest (which for a Chief is also made red) and deposited in the loft of a hut built for that purpose, and called bone house; each town has one of these; after remaining here one year or thereabouts, if he be a man of any note, they take the chest down, and in an assembly of relations and friends they weep once more over him, refresh the colour of the head, paint the box, and then deposit him to lasting oblivion.

An enemy and one who commits suicide is buried under the earth as one to be directly forgotten and unworthy the above ceremonial obsequies and mourning.

Jones [74] quotes one of the older writers, as follows, regarding the Natchez tribe:

Among the Natchez the dead were either inhumed or placed in tombs. These tombs were located within or very near their temples. They rested upon four forked sticks fixed fast in the ground, and were raised some three feet above the earth. About eight feet long and a foot and a half wide, they were prepared for the reception of a single corpse. After the body was placed upon it, a basket-work of twigs was woven around and covered with mud, an opening being left at the head, through which food was presented to the deceased. When the flesh had all rotted away, the bones were taken out, placed in a box made of canes, and then deposited in the temple. The common dead were mourned and lamented for a period of three days. Those who fell in battle were honored with a more protracted and grievous lamentation.

Bartram [75] gives a somewhat different account from Roman of burial among the Choctaws of Carolina:

The Chactaws pay their last duties and respect to the deceased in a very different manner. As soon as a person is dead, they erect a scaffold 18 or 20 feet high in a grove adjacent to the town, where they lay the corps, lightly covered with a mantle; here it is suffered to remain, visited and protected by the friends and relations, until the flesh becomes putrid, so as easily to part from the bones; then undertakers, who make it their business, carefully strip the flesh from the bones, wash and cleanse them, and when dry and purified by the air, having provided a curiously-wrought chest or coffin, fabricated of bones and splints, they place all the bones therein, which is deposited in the bone-house, a building erected for that purpose in every town; and when this house is full a general solemn funeral takes place; when the nearest kindred or friends of the deceased, on a day appointed, repair to the bone-house, take up the respective coffins, and, following one another in order of seniority, the nearest relations and connections attending their respective corps, and the multitude following after them, all as one family, with united voice of alternate allelujah and lamentation, slowly proceeding on to the place of general interment, when they place the coffins in order, forming a pyramid; [76*] and, lastly, cover all over with earth, which raises a conical hill or mount; when they return to town in order of solemn procession, concluding the day with a festival, which is called the feast of the dead.

Morgan [77] also alludes to this mode of burial:

The body of the deceased was exposed upon a bark scaffolding erected upon poles or secured upon the limbs of trees, where it was left to waste to a skeleton. After this had been effected by the process of decomposition in the open air, the bones were removed either to the former house of the deceased, or to a small bark house by its side, prepared for their reception. In this manner the skeletons of the whole family were preserved from generation to generation by the filial or parental affection of the living. After the lapse of a number of years, or in a season of public insecurity, or on the eve of abandoning a settlement, it was customary to collect these skeletons from the whole community around and consign them to a common resting-place.

To this custom, which is not confined to the Iroquois, is doubtless to be ascribed the burrows and bone-mounds which have been found in such numbers in various parts of the country. On opening these mounds the skeletons are usually found arranged in horizontal layers, a conical pyramid, those in each layer radiating from a common center. In other cases they are found placed promiscuously.

Dr. D. G. Brinton [78] likewise gives an account of the interment of collected bones:

East of the Mississippi nearly every nation was accustomed at stated periods—usually once in eight or ten years—to collect and clean the osseous remains of those of its number who had died in the intervening time, and inter them in one common sepulcher, lined with choice furs, and marked with a mound of wood, stone, or earth. Such is the origin of those immense tumuli filed with the mortal remains of nations and generations, which the antiquary, with irreverent curiosity, so frequently chances upon in all portions of our territory. Throughout Central America the same usage obtained in various localities, as early writers and existing monuments abundantly testify. Instead of interring the bones, were they those of some distinguished chieftain, they were deposited in the temples or the council-houses, usually in small chests of canes or splints. Such were the charnel-houses which the historians of De Soto's expedition so often mention, and these are the "arks" Adair and other authors who have sought to trace the decent of the Indians from the Jews have likened to that which the ancient Israelites bore with them in their migration.

A widow among the Tahkalis was obliged to carry the bones of her deceased husband wherever she went for four years, preserving them in such a casket, handsomely decorated with feathers (Rich. Arc. Exp., p. 200). The Caribs of the mainland adopted the custom for all, without exception. About a year after death the bones were cleaned, bleached, painted, wrapped in odorous balsams, placed in a wicker basket, and kept suspended from the door of their dwelling (Gumilla Hist. del Orinoco I., pp. 199, 202, 204). When the quantity of these heirlooms became burdensome they were removed to some inaccessible cavern and stowed away with reverential care.

George Catlin [79] describes what he calls the "Golgothas" of the Mandans:

There are several of these golgothas, or circles of twenty or thirty feet in diameter, and in the center of each ring or circle is a little mound of three feet high, on which uniformly rest two buffalo skulls (a male and female), and in the center of the little mound is erected "a medicine pole," of about twenty feet high, supporting many curious articles of mystery and superstition, which they suppose have the power of guarding and protecting this sacred arrangement.

Here, then, to this strange place do these people again resort to evince their further affections for the dead, not in groans and lamentations, however, for several years have cured the anguish, but fond affection and endearments are here renewed, and conversations are here held and cherished with the dead. Each one of these skulls is placed upon a bunch of wild sage, which has been pulled and placed under it. The wife knows, by some mark or resemblance, the skull of her husband or her child which lies in this group, and there seldom passes a day that she does not visit it with a dish of the best-cooked food that her wigwam affords, which she sets before the skull at night, and returns for the dish in the morning. As soon as it is discovered that the sage on which the skull rests is beginning to decay, the woman cuts a fresh bunch and places the skull carefully upon it, removing that which was under it.

Independent of the above-named duties, which draw the women to this spot, they visit it from inclination, and linger upon it to hold converse and company with the dead. There is scarcely an hour in a pleasant day but more or less of these women may be seen sitting or lying by the skull of their child or husband, talking to it in the most pleasant and endearing language that they can use (as they were wont to do in former days), and seemingly getting an answer back.

From these accounts it may be seen that the peculiar customs which have been described by the authors cited were not confined to any special tribe or area of country, although they do not appear to have prevailed among the Indians of the northwest coast, so far as known.

SUPERTERRENE AND AERIAL BURIAL IN CANOES.

The next mode of burial to be remarked is that of deposit in canoes, either supported on posts, on the ground, or swung from trees, and is common only to the tribes inhabiting the northwest coast.

The first example given relates to the Chinooks of Washington Territory, and may be found in Swan. [80]

> In this instance old Cartumhays, and old Mahar, a celebrated doctor, were the chief mourners, probably from being the smartest scamps among the relatives. Their duty was to prepare the canoe for the reception of the body. One of the largest and best the deceased had owned was then hauled into the woods, at some distance back of the lodge, after having been first thoroughly washed and scrubbed. Two large square holes were then cut in the bottom, at the bow and stern, for the twofold purpose of rendering the canoe unfit for further use, and therefore less likely to excite the cupidity of the whites (who are but too apt to help themselves to these depositories for the dead), and also to allow any rain to pass off readily.

> When the canoe was ready, the corpse, wrapped in blankets, was brought out, and laid in it on mats previously spread. All the wearing apparel was next put in beside the body, together with her trinkets, beads, little baskets, and various trifles she had prized. More blankets were then covered over the body, and mats smoothed over all. Next, a small canoe, which fitted into the large one, was placed, bottom up, over the corpse, and the whole then covered with mats. The canoe was

132

then raised up and placed on two parallel bars, elevated four or five feet from the ground, and supported by being inserted through holes mortised at the top of four stout posts previously firmly planted in the earth. Around these holes were then hung blankets, and all the cooking utensils of the deceased, pots, kettles, and pans, each with a hole punched through it, and all her crockery-ware, every piece of which was first cracked or broken, to render it useless; and then, when all was done, they left her to remain for one year, when the bones would be buried in a box in the earth directly under the canoe; but that, with all its appendages, would never be molested, but left to go to gradual decay.

They regard these canoes precisely as we regard coffins, and would no more think of using one than we would of using our own graveyard relics; and it is, in their view, as much of a desecration for a white man to meddle or interfere with these, to them, sacred mementoes, as it would be to us to have an Indian open the graves of our relatives. Many thoughtless white men have done this, and animosities have been thus occasioned.

Figure 23 represents this mode of burial.

F<small>IG</small>. 23.—Canoe Burial.

From a number of other examples, the following, relating to the Twanas, and furnished by the Rev. M. Eells, missionary to the Skokomish Agency, Washington Territory, is selected:

> The deceased was a woman about thirty or thirty-five years of age, dead of consumption. She died in the morning, and in the afternoon I went to the house to attend the funeral. She had then been placed in a Hudson's Bay Company's box for a coffin, which was about 3½ feet long, 1½ wide, and 1½ high. She was very poor when she died, owing to her disease, or she could not have been put in this box. A fire was burning near by, where a large number of her things had been consumed, and the rest was in three boxes near the coffin. Her mother sang the mourning song, sometimes with others, and often saying, "My daughter, my daughter, why did you die?" and similar words. The burial did not take place until the next day, and I was invited to go. It was an aerial burial in a canoe. The canoe was about 25 feet long. The posts, of old Indian layered boards, were about a foot wide. Holes

were cut in those, in which boards were placed, on which the canoe rested. One thing I noticed while this was done which was new to me, but the significance of which I did not learn. As fast as the holes were cut in the posts, green leaves were gathered and placed over the holes until the posts were put in the ground. The coffin-box and the three others containing her things were placed in the canoe and a roof of boards made over the central part, which was entirely covered with white cloth. The head part and the foot part of her bedstead were then nailed on to the posts, which front the water, and a dress nailed on each of these. After pronouncing the benediction, all left the hull and went to the beach except her father, mother, and brother, who remained ten or fifteen minutes, pounding on the canoe and mourning. They then came down and made a present to those persons who were there—a gun to one, a blanket to each of two or three others, and a dollar and a half to each of the rest, including myself, there being about fifteen persons present. Three or four of them then made short speeches, and we came home.

FIG. 24.—Twana Canoe-Burial.

The reason why she was buried thus is said to be because she is a prominent woman in the tribe. In about nine months it is expected that there will be a "*pot-latch*" or distribution of money near this place, and as each tribe shall come they will send a delegation of two or three men, who will carry a present and leave it at the grave; soon after that shall be done she will be buried in the ground. Shortly after her death both her father and mother cut off their hair as a sign of their grief.

Figure 24 is from a sketch kindly furnished by Mr. Eells, and represents the burial mentioned in his narrative.

The Clallams and Twanas, an allied tribe, have not always followed canoe-burial, as may be seen from the following account, also written by Mr. Eells, who gives the reasons why the original mode of disposing of the dead was abandoned. It is extremely interesting, and characterized by painstaking attention to detail:

I divide this subject into five periods, varying according to time, though they are somewhat intermingled.

(a) There are places where skulls and skeletons have been plowed up or still remain in the ground and near together, in such a way as to give good ground for the belief which is held by white residents in the region, that formerly persons were buried in the ground and in irregular cemeteries. I know of such places in Duce Waillops among the Twanas, and at Dungeness and Port Angeles among the Clallams. These graves were made so long ago that the Indians of the present day profess to have no knowledge as to who is buried in them, except that they believe, undoubtedly, that they are the graves of their ancestors. I do not know that any care has ever been exercised by any one in exhuming these skeletons so as to learn any particulars about them. It is possible, however, that these persons were buried according to the (b) or canoe method, and that time has buried them where they now are.

(b) Formerly when a person died the body was placed in the forks of two trees and left there. There was no particular cemetery, but the person was generally left near the place where the death occurred. The Skokomish Valley is said to have been full of canoes containing persons thus buried. What their customs were while burying, or what they placed around the dead, I am not informed but am told that they did not take as much care then of their dead as they do now. I am satisfied, however, that they then left some articles around the dead. An old resident informs me that the Clallam Indians always bury their dead in a sitting posture.

(c) About twenty years ago gold mines were discovered in British Columbia, and boats being scarce in the region, unprincipled white men took many of the canoes in which the Indian dead had been left, emptying them of their contents. This incensed the Indians and they changed their mode of burial somewhat by burying the dead in one place, placing them in boxes whenever they could obtain them, by building scaffolds for them instead of placing them in forks of trees, and in cutting their canoes so as to render them useless, when they were used as coffins or left by the side of the dead. The ruins of one such graveyard now remain about two miles from this agency. Nearly all the remains were removed a few years ago.

With this I furnish you the outlines of such graves which I have drawn. Fig. 25 shows that at present only one pair of posts remains.

I have supplied the other pair as they evidently were.

F_IG. 25.—Posts for Burial Canoes.

Figure 26 is a recent grave at another place. That part which is covered with board and cloth incloses the coffin which is on a scaffold.

F_IG. 26.—Tent on Scaffold.

As the Indians have been more in contact with the whites they have learned to bury in the ground, and this is the most common method at the present time. There are cemeteries everywhere where Indians have resided any length of time. After a person has died a coffin is made after the cheaper kinds of American ones, the body is placed in it, and also with it a number of articles, chiefly cloth or clothes, though occasionally money. I lately heard of a child being buried with a twenty-dollar gold piece in each hand and another in its month, but I am not able to vouch for the truth of it. As a general thing, money is too valuable with them for this purpose and there is too much temptation for some one to rob the grave when this is left in it.

(d) The grave is dug after the style of the whites and the coffin then placed in it. After it has been covered it is customary though not universal, to build some kind of an inclosure over it or around it in the shape of a small house, shed, lodge or fence. These are from 2 to 12 feet high, from 2 to 6 feet wide, and from 5 to 12 feet long. Some of these are so well inclosed that it is impossible to see within and some are quite open. Occasionally a window is placed in the front side. Sometimes these enclosures are covered with cloth, which is generally white, sometimes partly covered, and some have none. Around the grave, both outside and inside of the inclosure, various articles are placed, as guns, canoes, dishes, pails, cloth, sheets, blankets, beads, tubs, lamps, bows, mats, and occasionally a roughly-carved human image rudely painted. It is said that around and in the grave of one Clallam chief, buried a few years ago, $500 worth of such things were left. Most of these articles are cut or broken so as to render them valueless to man and to prevent their being stolen. Poles are also often erected, from 10 to 30 feet long, on which American flags, handkerchiefs, clothes, and cloths of various colors are hung. A few graves have nothing of this kind. On some graves these things are renewed every year or two. This depends mainly on the number of relatives living and the esteem in which they hold the deceased.

F_{IG}. 27.—House-Burial.

The belief exists that as the body decays spirits carry it away particle by particle to the spirit of the deceased in the spirit land, and also as these articles decay they are also carried away in a similar manner. I have never known of the placing food near a grave. Figures 27 and 28 will give you some idea of this class of graves. Figure 27 has a paling fence 12 feet square around it. Figure 28 is simply a frame over a grave where there is no enclosure.

F_{IG}. 28.—House-Burial.

(e) *Civilized mode.*—A few persons, of late, have fallen almost entirely into the American custom of burying, building a simple paling fence around it, but placing no articles around it; this is more especially true of the Clallams.

FUNERAL CEREMONIES.

In regard to the funeral ceremonies and mourning observances of sections (*a*) and (*b*) of the preceding subject I know nothing. In regard to (*c*) and (*d*), they begin to mourn, more especially the women, as soon as a person dies. Their mourning song consists principally of the sounds represented by the three English notes mi mi, do do, la la; those who attend the funeral are expected to bring some articles to place in the coffin or about the grave as a token of respect for the dead. The articles which I have seen for this purpose have been cloth of some kind; a small piece of cloth is returned by the mourners to the attendants as a token of remembrance. They bury much sooner after death than white persons do, generally as soon as they can obtain a coffin. I know of no other native funeral ceremonies. Occasionally before being taken to the grave, I have held Christian funeral ceremonies over them, and these services increase from year to year. One reason which has rendered them somewhat backward about having these funeral services is, that they are quite superstitions about going near the dead, fearing that the evil spirit which killed the deceased will enter the living and kill them also. Especially are they afraid of having children go near, being much more fearful of the effect of the evil spirit on them than on older persons.

MOURNING OBSERVANCES.

They have no regular period, so far as I know, for mourning, but often continue it after the burial, though I do not know that they often visit the grave. If they feel the loss very much, sometimes they will mourn nearly every day for several weeks; especially is this true when they meet an old friend who has not been seen since the funeral, or when they see an article owned by the deceased which they have not seen for a long time. The only other thing of which I think, which bears on this subject, is an idea they have, that before a person dies—it may be but a short time or it may be several months—a spirit from the spirit land comes and carries off the spirit of the individual to that place. There are those who profess to discover when this is done, and if by any of their incantations they can compel that spirit to return, the person will not die, but if they are not able, then the person will become dead at heart and in time die, though it may not be for six

140

months or even twelve. You will also find a little on this subject in a pamphlet which I wrote on the Twana Indians and which has recently been published by the Department of the Interior, under Prof. F. V. Hayden, United States Geologist.

George Gibbs [81] gives a most interesting account of the burial ceremonies of the Indians of Oregon and Washington Territory, which is here reproduced in its entirety, although it contains examples of other modes of burial besides that in canoes; but to separate the narrative would destroy the thread of the story:

The common mode of disposing of the dead among the fishing tribes was in canoes. These were generally drawn into the woods at some prominent point a short distance from the village, and sometimes placed between the forks of trees or raised from the ground on posts. Upon the Columbia River the Tsinūk had in particular two very noted cemeteries, a high isolated bluff about three miles below the mouth of the Cowlitz, called Mount Coffin, and one some distance above, called Coffin Rock. The former would appear not to have been very ancient. Mr. Broughton, one of Vancouver's lieutenants, who explored the river, makes mention only of *several* canoes at this place; and Lewis and Clarke, who noticed the mount, do not speak of them at all, but at the time of Captain Wilkes's expedition it is conjectured that there were at least 3,000. A fire caused by the carelessness of one of his party destroyed the whole, to the great indignation of the Indians.

Captain Belcher, of the British ship Sulphur, who visited the river in 1839, remarks: "In the year 1836 [1826] the small-pox made great ravages, and it was followed a few years since by the ague. Consequently Corpse Island and Coffin Mount, as well as the adjacent shores, were studded not only with canoes, but at the period of our visit the skulls and skeletons were strewed about in all directions." This method generally prevailed on the neighboring coasts, as at Shoal Water Bay, &c. Farther up the Columbia, as at the Cascades, a different form was adopted, which is thus described by Captain Clarke:

"About half a mile below this house, in a very thick part of the woods, is an ancient Indian burial-place; it consists of eight vaults, made of pine cedar boards, closely connected, about 8 feet square and 6 in height, the top securely covered with wide boards, sloping a little, so as to convey off the rain. The direction of all these is east and west, the door being on the eastern side, and partially stopped with wide boards, decorated with rude pictures of men and other animals. On entering we found in some of them four dead bodies, carefully wrapped in skins, tied with cords of grass and bark, lying on a mat in a direction east and west; the other vaults contained only bones, which in some of them were piled to a height of 4 feet; on the tops of the vaults and on poles attached to them hung brass kettles and frying-pans with holes in their bottoms, baskets, bowls, sea-shells, skins, pieces of cloth, hair bags of trinkets, and small bones, the offerings of friendship or affection, which have been saved by a pious veneration from the ferocity of war or the more dangerous temptation of individual gain. The whole of the walls as well as the door were decorated with strange figures cut and painted on them, and besides these were several wooden images of men, some of them so old and decayed as to have almost lost their shape, which were all placed against the sides of the vault. These images, as well as those in the houses we have lately seen, do not appear to be at all the objects of adoration in this place; they were most probably intended as resemblances of those whose decease they indicate, and when we observe them in houses they occupy the most conspicuous part, but are treated more like ornaments than objects of worship. Near the vaults which are still standing are the remains of others on the ground, completely rotted and covered with moss; and as they are formed of the most durable pine and cedar timber, there is every appearance that for a very long series of years this retired spot has been the depository for the Indians near this place."

Another depository of this kind upon an island in the river a few miles above gave it the name of Sepulcher Inland. The *Watlala*, a tribe of the Upper Tsinūk, whose burial place is here described, are now nearly extinct; but a number of the sepulchers still remain in different states of preservation. The position of the body, as noticed by Clarke, is, I believe, of universal observance, the head being always placed to the west. The reason assigned to me is that the road to the *mé-mel-ūs-illa-hee*, the country of the dead, is toward the west, and if they place them otherwise they would be confused. East of the Cascade Mountains the tribes whose habits are equestrian, and who use canoes only for ferriage or transportation purposes, bury their dead, usually heaping over them piles of stones, either to mark the spot or to prevent the bodies from being exhumed by the prairie wolf. Among the Yakamas we saw many of their graves placed in conspicuous points of the basaltic walls which line the lower valleys, and designated by a clump of poles planted over them, from which fluttered various articles of dress. Formerly these prairie tribes killed horses over the graves—a custom now falling into disuse in consequence of the teachings of the whites.

Upon Puget Sound all the forms obtain in different localities. Among the Makah of Cape Flattery the graves are covered with a sort of box, rudely constructed of boards, and elsewhere on the Sound the same method is adopted in some cases, while in others the bodies are placed on elevated scaffolds. As a general thing, however, the Indians upon the water placed the dead in canoes, while those at a distance from it buried them. Most of the graves are surrounded with strips of cloth, blankets, and other articles of property. Mr. Cameron, an English gentleman residing at Esquimalt Harbor, Vancouver Island, informed me that on his place there were graves having at each corner a large stone, the interior space filled with rubbish. The origin of these was unknown to the present Indians.

The distinctions of rank or wealth in all cases were very marked; persons of no consideration and slaves being buried with very little care or respect. Vancouver, whose attention was particularly attracted to their methods of disposing of the dead, mentions that at Port Discovery he saw baskets suspended to the trees containing the skeletons of young children, and, what is not easily explained, small square boxes, containing, apparently, food. I do not think that any of these tribes place articles of food with the dead, nor have I been able to learn from living Indians that they formerly followed that practice. What he took for such I do not understand. He also mentions seeing in the same place a cleared space recently burned over, in which the skulls and bones of a number lay among the ashes. The practice of burning the dead exists in parts of California and among the Tshimsyan of Fort Simpson. It is also pursued by the "Carriers" of New California, but no intermediate tribes, to my knowledge, follow it. Certainly those of the Sound do not at present.

It is clear from Vancouver's narrative that some great epidemic had recently passed through the country, as manifested by the quantity of human remains uncared for and exposed at the time of his visit, and very probably the Indians, being afraid, had buried a house, in which the inhabitants had perished with the dead in it. This is frequently done. They almost invariably remove from any place where sickness has prevailed, generally destroying the house also.

At Penn Cove Mr. Whidbey, one of Vancouver's officers, noticed several sepulchers formed exactly like a sentry-box. Some of them were open, and contained the skeletons of many young children tied up in baskets. The smaller bones of adults were likewise noticed, but not one of the limb bones was found, which gave rise to an opinion that these, by the living inhabitants of the neighborhood, were appropriated to useful purposes, such as pointing their arrows, spears, or other weapons.

F<small>IG</small>. 29.—Canoe Burial.

It is hardly necessary to say that such a practice is altogether foreign to Indian character. The bones of the adults had probably been removed and buried elsewhere. The corpses of children are variously disposed of; sometimes by suspending them, at others by placing in the hollows of trees. A cemetery devoted to infants is, however, an unusual occurrence. In cases of chiefs or men of note much pomp was used in the accompaniments of the rite. The canoes were of great size and value—the war or state canoes of the deceased. Frequently one was inverted over that holding the body, and in one instance, near Shoalwater Bay, the corpse was deposited in a small canoe, which again was placed in a larger one and covered with a third. Among the *Tsinūk* and *Tsìhalis* the *tamahno-ūs* board of the owner was placed near him. The Puget Sound Indians do not make these *tamahno-ūs* boards, but they sometimes constructed effigies of their chiefs, resembling the person as nearly as possible, dressed in his usual costume, and wearing the articles of which he was fond. One of these, representing the Skagit chief Sneestum, stood very conspicuously upon a high bank on the eastern side of Whidbey Island. The figures observed by Captain Clarke at the Cascades were either of this description or else the carved posts which had ornamented the interior of the houses of the deceased, and were connected with the superstition of the *tamahno-ūs*. The most valuable articles of property were put into or hung up around the grave, being first carefully rendered unserviceable, and the living family were literally stripped to do honor to the dead. No little self-denial must have been practiced in parting with articles so precious, but those interested frequently had the least to say on the subject. The graves of women were distinguished by a cap, a Kamas stick, or other implement of their occupation, and by articles of dress.

Slaves were killed in proportion to the rank and wealth of the deceased. In some instances they were starved to death, or even tied to the dead body and left to perish thus horribly. At present this practice has been almost entirely given up, but till within a very few years it was not uncommon. A case which occurred in 1850 has been already mentioned. Still later, in 1853, Toke, a Tsinūk chief living at Shoalwater Bay, undertook to kill a slave girl belonging to his daughter, who, in dying, had requested that this might be done. The woman fled, and was found by some citizens in the woods half starved. Her master attempted to reclaim her, but was soundly thrashed and warned against another attempt.

It was usual in the case of chiefs to renew or repair for a considerable length of time the materials and ornaments of the burial-place. With the common class of persons family pride or domestic affection was satisfied with the gathering together of the bones after the flesh had decayed and wrapping them in a new mat. The violation of the grave was always regarded as an offense of the first magnitude and provoked severe revenge. Captain Belcher remarks: "Great secrecy is observed in all their burial ceremonies, partly from fear of Europeans, and as among themselves they will instantly punish by death any violation of the tomb or wage war if perpetrated by another tribe, so they are inveterate and tenaceously bent on revenge should they discover that any act of the kind has been perpetrated by a white man. It is on record that part of the crew of a vessel on her return to this port (the Columbia) suffered because a person who belonged to her (but not then in her) was known to have taken a skull, which, from the process of flattening, had become an object of curiosity." He adds, however, that at the period of his visit to the river "the skulls and skeletons were scattered about in all directions; and as I was on most of their positions unnoticed by the natives, I suspect the feeling does not extend much beyond their relatives, and then only till decay has destroyed body, goods, and chattels. The chiefs, no doubt, are watched, as their canoes are repainted, decorated, and greater care taken by placing them in sequestered spots."

The motive for sacrificing or destroying property on occasion of death will be referred to in treating of their religious ideas. Wailing for the dead is continued for a long time, and it seems to be rather a ceremonial performance than an act of spontaneous grief. The duty, of course, belongs to the woman, and the early morning is usually chosen for the purpose. They go out alone to some place a little distant from the lodge or camp and in a loud, sobbing voice repeat a sort of stereotyped formula; as, for instance, a mother, on the loss of her child, "*A seahb shed-da bud-dah ah ta bud! ad-de-dah*," "Ah chief!" "My child dead, alas!" When in dreams they see any of their deceased friends this lamentation is renewed.

With most of the Northwest Indians it was quite common, as mentioned by Mr. Gibbs, to kill or bury with the dead a living slave, who, failing to die within three days, was strangled by another slave; but the custom has also prevailed among other tribes and peoples, in many cases the individuals offering themselves as voluntary sacrifices. Bancroft states that—

In Panama, Nata, and some other districts, when a cacique died, those of his concubines that loved him enough, those that he loved ardently and so appointed, as well as certain servants, killed themselves and were interred with him. This they did in order that they might wait upon him in the land of spirits.

It is well known to all readers of history to what an extreme this revolting practice has prevailed in Mexico, South America, and Africa.

AQUATIC BURIAL.

As a confirmed rite or ceremony, this mode of disposing of the dead has never been followed by any of our North American Indians, although occasionally the dead have been disposed of by sinking in springs or water-courses, by throwing into the sea, or by setting afloat in canoes. Among the nations of antiquity the practice was not uncommon, for we are informed that the Ichthyophagi, or fish-eaters, mentioned by Ptolemy, living in a region bordering on the Persian Gulf, invariably committed their dead to the sea, thus repaying the obligations they had incurred to its inhabitants. The Lotophagians did the same, and the Hyperboreans, with a commendable degree of forethought for the survivors, when ill or about to die, threw themselves into the sea. The burial of Balder "the beautiful," it may be remembered, was in a highly decorated ship, which was pushed down to the sea, set on fire, and committed to the waves. The Itzas of Guatemala, living on the islands of Lake Peten, according to Bancroft, are said to have thrown their dead into the lake for want of room. The Indians of Nootka Sound and the Chinooks were in the habit of thus getting rid of their dead slaves, and, according to Timberlake, the Cherokees of Tennessee "seldom bury the dead, but throw them into the river."

The Alibamans, as they were called by Bossu, denied the rite of sepulture to suicides; they were looked upon as cowards, and their bodies thrown into a river. The Rev. J. G. Wood [82] states that the Obongo or African tribe takes the body to some running stream, the course of which has been previously diverted. A deep grave is dug in the bed of the stream, the body placed in it, and covered over carefully. Lastly, the stream is restored to its original course, so that all traces of the grave are soon lost.

The Kavague also bury their common people, or wanjambo, by simply sinking the body in some stream.

Historians inform us that Alaric was buried in a manner similar to that employed by the Obongo, for in 410, at Cosença, a town of Calabria, the Goths turned aside the course of the river Vasento, and having made a grave in the midst of its bed, where its course was most rapid, they interred their king with a prodigious amount of wealth and riches. They then caused the river to resume its regular course, and destroyed all persons who had been concerned in preparing this romantic grave.

A later example of water-burial is that afforded by the funeral of De Soto. Dying in 1542, his remains were inclosed in a wooden chest well weighted, and committed to the turbid and tumultuous waters of the Mississippi.

After a careful search for well-authenticated instances of burial, aquatic and semi-aquatic, among North American Indians, but two have been found, which are here given. The first relates to the Gosh-Utes, and is by Capt. J. H. Simpson: [83]

> Skull Valley, which is a part of the Great Salt Lake Desert, and which we have crossed to-day, Mr. George W. Bean, my guide over this route last fall, says derives its name from the number of skulls which have been found in it, and which have arisen from the custom of the Goshute Indians burying their dead in springs, which they sank with stones or keep down with sticks. He says he has actually seen the Indians bury their dead in this way near the town of Provo, where he resides.

As corroborative of this statement, Captain Simpson mentions in another part of the volume that, arriving at a spring one evening, they were obliged to dig out the skeleton of an Indian from the mud at the bottom before using the water.

F<small>IG</small>. 30.—Mourning Cradle.

This peculiar mode of burial is entirely unique, so far as known, and but from the well-known probity of the relator might well be questioned, especially when it is remembered that in the country spoken of water is quite scarce and Indians are careful not to pollute the streams or springs near which they live. Conjecture seems useless to establish a reason for this disposition of the dead, unless we are inclined to attribute it to the natural indolence of the savage, or a desire to poison the springs for white persons.

The second example is by George Catlin,[84] and relates to the Chinook:

    *   *   *   This little cradle has a strap which passes over the woman's forehead whilst the cradle rides on her back, and if the child dies during its subjection to this rigid mode, its cradle becomes its coffin, forming a little canoe, in which it lies floating on the water in some sacred pool, where they are often in the habit of fastening their canoes containing the dead bodies of the old and young, or, which in often the case, elevated into the branches of trees, where their bodies are left to decay and their bones to dry whilst they are bandaged in many skins and curiously packed in their canoes, with paddles to propel and ladles to bale them out, and provisions to last and pipes to

149

smoke as they are performing their "long journey after death to their contemplated hunting grounds," which these people think is to be performed in their canoes.

Figure 30, after Catlin, is a representation of a mourning-cradle. Figure 31 represents the sorrowing mother committing the body of her dead child to the mercy of the elements.

F$_{IG}$. 31.—Launching the Burial Cradle.

LIVING SEPULCHERS.

This is a term quaintly used by the learned M. Pierre Muret to express the devouring of the dead by birds and animals or the surviving friends and relatives. Exposure of the dead to animals and birds has already been mentioned, but in the absence of any positive proof, it is not believed that the North American Indians followed the custom, although cannibalism may have prevailed to a limited extent. It is true that a few accounts are given by authors, but these are considered apochryphal in character, and the one mentioned is only offered to show how credulous were the early writers on American natives.

That such a means of disposing of the dead was not in practice is somewhat remarkable when we take into consideration how many analogies been found in comparing old and new world funeral observances, and the statements made by Bruhier, Lafitau, Muret, and others, who give a number of examples of this peculiar mode of burial.

For instance, the Tartars sometimes ate their dead, and the Massagetics, Padæans, Derbices, and Effedens did the same, having previously strangled the aged and mixed their flesh with mutton. Horace and Tertullian both affirm that the Irish and ancient Britons devoured the dead, and Lafitau remarks that certain Indians of South America did the same, esteeming this mode of disposal more honorable and much to be preferred than to rot and be eaten by worms.

J. G. Wood, in his work already quoted, states that the Fans of Africa devour their dead, but this disposition is followed only for the common people, the kings and chiefs being buried with much ceremony.

The following extract is from Lafitau: [85]

> Dans l'Amérique Méridionale quelque Peuples décharnent les corps de leurs Guerriers et les mangent leurs chairs, ainsi que je viens de le dire, et après les avoir consumées, ils conservent pendant quelque temps leurs cadavres avec respect dans leurs Cabanes, et il portent ces squeletes dans les combats en guise d'Etendard, pour ranimer leur courage par cette vue et inspirer de la terreur à leurs ennemis.
> * * *
>
> Il est vrai qu'il y en a qui font festin des cadavres de leurs parens; mais il est faux qu'elles les mettent à mort dans leur vieillesse, pour avoir le plaisir de se nourrir de leur chair, et d'en faire un repas. Quelques Nations de l'Amérique Méridionale, qui ont encore cette coutume de manger les corps morts de leurs parens, n'en usent ainsi que par piété, piété mal entenduë à la verité, mais piété colorée néanmoins par quelque ombre de raison; car ils croyent leur donner

une sépulture bien plus honorable.

To the credit of our savages, this barbarous and revolting practice is not believed to have been practiced by them.

MOURNING, SACRIFICE, FEASTS, FOOD, DANCES, SONGS, GAMES, POSTS, FIRES, AND SUPERSTITIONS IN CONNECTION WITH BURIAL.

The above subjects are coincident with burial, and some of them, particularly mourning, have been more or less treated of in this paper, yet it may be of advantage to here give a few of the collected examples, under separate heads.

MOURNING.

One of the most carefully described scenes of mourning at the death of a chief of the Crows is related in the life of Beckwourth, [86] who for many years lived among this people, finally attaining great distinction as a warrior.

> I dispatched a herald to the village to inform them of the head chief's death, and then, burying him according to his directions, we slowly proceeded homewards. My very soul sickened at the contemplation of the scenes that would be enacted at my arrival. When we drew in sight of the village, we found every lodge laid prostrate. We entered amid shrieks, cries, and yells. Blood was streaming from every conceivable part of the bodies of all who were old enough to comprehend their loss. Hundreds of fingers were dismembered; hair torn from the head lay in profusion about the paths; wails and moans in every direction assailed the ear, where unrestrained joy had a few hours before prevailed. This fearful mourning lasted until evening of the next day.

*   *   *

A herald having been dispatched to our other villages to acquaint them with the death of our head chief, and request them to assemble at the Rose Bud, in order to meet our village and devote themselves to a general time of mourning, there met, in conformity to the summons, over ten thousand Crows at the place indicated. Such a scene of disorderly, vociferous mourning, no imagination can conceive nor any pen portray. Long Hair cut off a large roll of his hair; a thing he was never known to do before. The cutting and hacking of human flesh exceeded all my previous experience; fingers were dismembered as readily as twigs, and blood was poured out like water. Many of the warriors would cut two gashes nearly the entire length of their arm; then, separating the skin from the flesh at one end, would grasp it in their other hand, and rip it asunder to the shoulder. Others would carve various devices upon their breasts and shoulders, and raise the skin in the same manner to make the scars show to advantage after the wound was healed. Some of their mutilations were ghastly, and my heart sickened to look at them, but they would not appear to receive any pain from them.

It should be remembered that many of Beckwourth's statements are to be taken *cum grana salis*.

From I. L. Mahan, United States Indian agent for the Chippewas of Lake Superior, Red Cliff, Wisconsin, the following detailed account of mourning has been received:

There is probably no people that exhibit more sorrow and grief for their dead than they. The young widow mourns the loss of her husband; by day as by night she is heard silently sobbing; she is a constant visitor to the place of rest; with the greatest reluctance will she follow the raised camp. The friends and relatives of the young mourner will incessantly devise methods to distract her mind from the thought of her lost husband. She refuses nourishment, but as nature is exhausted she is prevailed upon to partake of food; the supply is scant, but on every occasion the best and largest proportion is deposited upon the grave of her husband. In the mean time the female relatives of the deceased have, according to custom, submitted to her charge a parcel made up of different cloths ornamented with bead-work and eagle's feathers, which she is charged to keep by her side—the place made vacant by the demise of her husband—a reminder of her widowhood. She is therefore for a term of twelve moons not permitted to wear any finery, neither is she permitted to slicken up and comb her head; this to avoid attracting attention. Once in a while a female relative of deceased, commiserating with her grief and sorrow, will visit her and voluntarily proceed to comb out the long-neglected and matted hair. With a jealous eye a vigilant watch is kept over her conduct during the term of her widowhood, yet she is allowed the privilege to marry, any time during her widowhood, an unmarried brother or cousin, or a person of the same *Dodem* [*sic*] (family mark) of her husband.

At the expiration of her term, the vows having been faithfully performed and kept, the female relatives of deceased assemble and, with greetings commensurate to the occasion, proceed to wash her face, comb her hair, and attire her person with new apparel, and otherwise demonstrating the release from her vow and restraint. Still she has not her entire freedom. If she will still refuse to marry a relative of the deceased and will marry another, she then has to purchase her freedom by giving a certain amount of goods and whatever else she might have manufactured during her widowhood in anticipation of the future now at hand. Frequently, though, during widowhood the vows are disregarded and an inclination to flirt and play courtship or form an alliance of marriage outside of the relatives of the deceased is being indulged, and when discovered the widow is set upon by the female relatives, her slick braided hair is shorn close up to the back of her neck, all her apparel and trinkets are torn from her person, and a quarrel frequently results fatally to some member of one or the other side.

Thomas L. McKenney [87] gives a description of the Chippewa widow which differs slightly from the one above:

I have noticed several women here carrying with them rolls of clothing. On inquiring what these imported, I learn that they *are widows* who carry them, and that these are badges of mourning. It is indispensable, when a woman of the Chippeway Nation loses her husband, for her to take of her best apparel—and the whole of it is not worth a dollar—and roll it up, and confine it by means of her husband's sashes; and if he had ornaments, these are generally put on the top of the roll, and around it is wrapped a piece of cloth. This bundle is called her husband, and it is expected that she is never to be seen without it. If she walks out she takes it with her; if she sits down in her lodge, she places it by her side. This badge of widowhood and of mourning the widow is compelled to carry with her until some of her late husband's family shall call and take it away, which is done when they think she has mourned long enough, and which is generally at the expiration of a year. She is then, but not before, released from her mourning, and at liberty to marry again. She has the privilege to take this husband to the family of the deceased and leave it, but this is considered indecorous, and is seldom done. Sometimes a brother of the deceased takes the widow for his wife at the grave of her husband, which is done by a ceremony of walking her over it. And this he has a right to do; and when this is done she is not required to go into mourning; or, if she chooses, she has the right *to go to him*, and he is *bound* to support her.

I visited a lodge to-day, where I saw one of these badges. The size varies according to the quantity of clothing which the widow may happen to have. It is expected of her to put up her *best* and wear her *worst*. The "*husband*" I saw just now was 30 inches high and 18 inches in circumference.

I was told by the interpreter that he knew a woman who had been left to mourn after this fashion for years, none of her husband's family calling for the badge or token of her grief. At a certain time it was told her that some of her husband's family were passing, and she was advised to speak to them on the subject. She did so, and told them she had mourned long and was poor; that she had no means to buy clothes, and her's being all in the mourning badge, and sacred, could not be touched. She expressed a hope that her request might not be interpreted into a wish to marry; it was only made that she might be placed in a situation to get some clothes. She got for answer, that "they were going to Mackinac, and would think of it." They left her in this state of uncertainty, but on returning, and finding her faithful still, they took her "husband" and presented her with clothing of various kinds. Thus was she rewarded for her constancy and made comfortable.

The Choctaw widows mourn by never combing their hair for the term of their grief, which is generally about a year. The Chippeway men mourn by painting their faces black.

I omitted to mention that when presents are going round, the badge of mourning, this "*husband*" comes in for an equal share, as if it were the living husband.

A Chippeway mother, on losing her child, prepares an image of it in the best manner she is able, and dresses it as she did her living child, and fixes it in the kind of cradle I have referred to, and goes through the ceremonies of nursing it as if it were alive, by dropping little particles of food in the direction of its mouth, and giving it of whatever the living child partook. This ceremony also is generally observed for a year.

Figure 32 represents the Chippewa widow holding in her arms the substitute for the dead husband.

F_{IG}. 32.—Chippewa Widow.

The substitution of a reminder for the dead husband, made from rags, furs, and other articles, is not confined alone to the Chippewas, other tribes having the same custom. In some instances the widows are obliged to carry around

156

with them, for a variable period, a bundle containing the bones of the deceased consort.

Similar observances, according to Bancroft, [88] were followed by some of the Central American tribes of Indians, those of the Sambos and Mosquitos being as follows:

> The widow was bound to supply the grave of her husband for a year, after which she took up the bones and carried them with her for another year, at last placing them upon the roof of her house, and then only was she allowed to marry again.

> On returning from the grave the property of the deceased is destroyed, the cocoa palms being cut down, and all who have taken part in the funeral undergo a lustration in the river. Relatives cut off the hair, the men leaving a ridge along the middle from the nape of the neck to the forehead. Widows, according to some old writers, after supplying the grave with food for a year take up the bones and carry them on the back in the daytime, sleeping with them at night for another year, after which they are placed at the door or upon the house-top. On the anniversary of deaths, friends of the deceased hold a feast, called *seekroe*, at which large quantities of liquor are drained to his memory. Squier, who witnessed the ceremonies on an occasion of this kind, says that males and females were dressed in *ule* cloaks fantastically painted black and white, while their faces were correspondingly streaked with red and yellow, and they performed a slow walk around, prostrating themselves at intervals and calling loudly upon the dead and tearing the ground with their hands. At no other time is the departed referred to, the very mention of his name being superstitiously avoided. Some tribes extend a thread from the house of death to the grave, carrying it in a straight line over every obstacle. Fröebel states that among the Woolwas all property of the deceased is buried with him, and that both husband and wife cut the hair and burn the hut on the death of either, placing a gruel of maize upon the grave for a certain time.

Benson [89] gives the following account of the Choctaws' funeral ceremonies, embracing the disposition of the body, mourning feast and dance:

> Their funeral is styled by them "the last cry."

> When the husband dies the friends assemble, prepare the grave, and place the corpse in it, but do not fill it up. The gun, bow and arrows,

hatchet, and knife are deposited in the grave. Poles are planted at the head and the foot, upon which flags are placed; the grave is then inclosed by pickets driven in the ground. The funeral ceremonies now begin, the widow being the chief mourner. At night and morning she will go to the grave and pour forth the most piteous cries and wailings. It is not important that any other member of the family should take any very active part in the "cry," though they do participate to some extent.

The widow wholly neglects her toilet, while she daily goes to the grave during one entire moon from the date when the death occurred. On the evening of the last day of the moon the friends all assemble at the cabin of the disconsolate widow, bringing provisions for a sumptuous feast, which consists of corn and jerked beef boiled together in a kettle. While the supper is preparing the bereaved wife goes to the grave and pours out, with unusual vehemence, her bitter wailings and lamentations. When the food is thoroughly cooked the kettle is taken from the fire and placed in the center of the cabin, and the friends gather around it, passing the buffalo-horn spoon from hand to hand and from mouth to mouth till all have been bountifully supplied. While supper is being served, two of the oldest men of the company quietly withdraw and go to the grave and fill it up, taking down the flags. All then join in a dance, which not unfrequently is continued till morning; the widow does not fail to unite in the dance, and to contribute her part to the festivities of the occasion. This is the "*last cry*," the days of mourning are ended, and the widow is now ready to form another matrimonial alliance. The ceremonies are precisely the same when a man has lost his wife, and they are only slightly varied when any other member of the family has died. (Slaves were buried without ceremonies.)

SACRIFICE.

Some examples of human sacrifice have already been given in connection with another subject, but it is thought others might prove interesting. The first relates to the Natchez of Louisiana. [90]

When their sovereign died he was accompanied in the grave by his wives and by several of his subjects. The lesser Suns took care to follow the same custom. The law likewise condemned every Natchez to death who had married a girl of the blood of the Suns as soon as she was expired. On this occasion I must tell you the history of an Indian who was noways willing to submit to this law. His name was *Elteacteal*; he contracted an alliance with the Suns, but the consequences which this honor brought along with it had like to have proved very unfortunate to him. His wife fell sick; as soon as he saw her at the point of death he fled, embarked in a piragua on the *Mississippi*, and came to New Orleans. He put himself under the protection of M. de Bienville, the then governor, and offered to be his huntsman. The governor accepted his services, and interested himself for him with the Natchez, who declared that he had nothing more to fear, because the ceremony was past, and he was accordingly no longer a lawful prize.

Elteacteal, being thus assured, ventured to return to his nation, and, without settling among them, he made several voyages thither. He happened to be there when the Sun called the *Stung Serpent*, brother to the Great Sun, died. He was a relative of the late wife of *Elteacteal*, and they resolved to make him pay his debt. M. de Bienville had been recalled to France, and the sovereign of the Natchez thought that the protector's absence had annulled the reprieve granted to the protected person, and accordingly he caused him to be arrested. As soon as the poor fellow found himself in the hut of the grand chief of war, together with the other victims destined to be sacrificed to the *Stung Serpent*, he gave vent to the excess of his grief. The favorite wife of the late Son, who was likewise to be sacrificed, and who saw the preparations for her death with firmness, and seemed impatient to rejoin her husband, hearing *Elteacteal's* complaints and groans, said to him: "Art thou no warrior?" He answered, "Yes: I am one." "However," said she, "thou cryest; life is dear to thee, and as that is the case, it is not good that thou shouldst go along with us; go with the women." *Elteacteal* replied: "True; life is dear to me. It would be well if I walked yet on earth till to the death of the Great Sun, and I would die with him." "Go thy way," said the favorite, "it is not fit thou shouldst go with us, and that thy heart should remain behind on earth. Once more, get away, and let me see thee no more."

Elteacteal did not stay to hear this order repeated to him; he disappeared like lightning; three old women, two of which were his relatives, offered to pay his debt; their age and their infirmities had disgusted them of life; none of them had been able to use their legs for a great while. The hair of the two that were related to *Elteacteal* was no more gray than those of women of fifty-five years in France. The other old woman was a hundred and twenty years old, and had very white hair, which is a very uncommon thing among the Indians. None of the three had a quite wrinkled skin. They were dispatched in the evening, one at the door of the *Stung Serpent*, and the other two upon the place before the temple.   *   *   *   A cord is fastened round their necks with a slip-knot, and eight men of their relations strangle them by drawing, four one way and four the other. So many are not necessary, but as they acquire nobility by such executions, there are always more than are wanting, and the operation is performed in an instant. The generosity of these women gave *Elteacteal* life again, acquired him the degree of *considered*, and cleared his honor, which he had sullied by fearing death. He remained quiet after that time, and taking advantage of what he had learned during his stay among the French, he became a juggler and made use of his knowledge to impose upon his countrymen.

The morning after this execution they made everything ready for the convoy, and the hour being come, the great master of the ceremonies appeared at the door of the hut, adorned suitably to his quality. The victims who were to accompany the deceased prince into the mansion of the spirits came forth; they consisted of the favorite wife of the deceased, of his second wife, his chancellor, his physician, his hired man, that is, his first servant, and of some old women.

The favorite went to the Great Sun, with whom there were several Frenchmen, to take leave of him; she gave orders for the Suns of both sexes that were her children to appear, and spoke to the following effect:

"Children, this is the day on which I am to tear myself from you (*sic*) arms and to follow your father's steps, who waits for me in the country of the spirits; if I were to yield to your tears I would injure my love and fail in my duty. I have done enough for you by bearing you next to my heart, and by suckling you with my breasts. You that are descended of his blood and fed by my milk, ought you to shed tears? Rejoice rather that you are *Suns* and warriors; you are bound to give examples of firmness and valor to the whole nation: go, my children, I have provided for all your wants, by procuring you friends; my friends and those of your father are yours too; I leave you amidst them; they are the French; they are tender-hearted and generous; make yourselves worthy of their esteem by not degenerating from your race; always act openly with them and never implore them with meanness.

"And you, Frenchmen," added she, turning herself towards our officers, "I recommend my orphan children to you; they will know no other fathers than you; you ought to protect them."

After that she got up; and, followed by her troop, returned to her husband's hut with a surprising firmness.

A noble woman came to join herself to the number of victims of her own accord, being engaged by the friendship she bore the *Stung Serpent* to follow him into the other world. The Europeans called her the *haughty* lady, on account of her majestic deportment and her proud air, and because she only frequented the company of the most distinguished Frenchmen. They regretted her much, because she had the knowledge of several simples with which she had saved the lives of many of our sick. This moving sight filled our people with grief and horror. The favorite wife of the deceased rose up and spoke to them with a smiling countenance: "I die without fear;" said she, "grief does not embitter my last hours. I recommend my children to you; whenever you see them, noble Frenchmen, remember that you have loved their father, and that he was till death a true and sincere friend of your nation, whom he loved more than himself. The disposer of life has been pleased to call him, and I shall soon go and join him; I shall tell him that I have seen your hearts moved at the sight of his corps; do not be grieved; we shall be longer friends in the *country of the spirits* than here, because we do not die there again."91*

These words forced tears from the eyes of all the French; they were obliged to do all they could to prevent the Great Sun from killing himself, for he was inconsolable at the death of his brother, upon whom he was used to lay the weight of government, he being great chief of war of the Natches, i.e. generalissimo of their armies; that prince grew furious by the resistance he met with; he held his gun by the barrel, and the Sun, his presumptive heir, held it by the lock, and caused the powder to fall out of the pan; the hut was full of Suns, Nobles, and Honorables 92* but the French raised their spirits again, by hiding all the arms belonging to the sovereign, and filling the barrel of his gun with water, that it might be unfit for use for some time.

As soon as the Suns saw their sovereign's life in safety, they thanked the French, by squeezing their hands, but without speaking; a most profound silence reigned throughout, for grief and awe kept in bounds the multitude that were present.

The wife of the Great Sun was seized with fear during this transaction. She was asked whether she was ill, and she answered aloud, "Yes, I am"; and added with a lower voice, "If the Frenchmen go out of this hut, my husband dies and all the Natches will die with him; stay, then, brave Frenchmen, because your words are as powerful as arrows; besides, who could have ventured to do what you have done? But you are his true friends and those of his brother." Their laws obliged the Great Sun's wife to follow her husband in the grave; this was doubtless the cause of her fears; and likewise the gratitude towards the French, who interested themselves in behalf of his life, prompted her to speak in the above-mentioned manner.

The Great Sun gave his hand to the officers, and said to them: "My friends, my heart is so overpowered with grief that, though my eyes were open, I have not taken notice that you have been standing all this while, nor have I asked you to sit down; but pardon the excess of my affliction."

The Frenchmen told him that he had no need of excuses; that they were going to leave him alone, but that they would cease to be his friends unless he gave orders to light the fires again, [93*] lighting his own before them; and that they should not leave him till his brother was buried.

He took all the Frenchmen by the hands, and said: "Since all the chiefs and noble officers will have me stay on earth, I will do it; I will not kill myself; let the fires be lighted again immediately, and I'll wait till death joins me to my brother; I am already old, and till I die I shall walk with the French; had it not been for them I should have gone with my brother, and all the roads would have been covered with dead bodies."

Improbable as this account may appear, it has nevertheless been credited by some of the wisest and most careful of ethnological writers, and its seeming appearance of romance disappears when the remembrance of similar ceremonies among Old World peoples comes to our minds.

An apparently well-authenticated case of attempted burial sacrifice is described by Miss A. J. Allen, [94] and refers to the Wascopums, of Oregon.

At length, by meaning looks and gestures rather than words, it was found that the chief had determined that the deceased boy's friend, who had been his companion in hunting the rabbit, snaring the pheasant, and fishing in the streams, was to be his companion to the spirit land; his son should not be deprived of his associate in the strange world to which he had gone; that associate should perish by the hand of his father, and be conveyed with him to the dead-house. This receptacle was built on a long, black rock in the center of the Columbia River, around which, being so near the falls, the current was amazingly rapid. It was thirty feet in length, and perhaps half that in breadth, completely enclosed and sodded except at one end, where was a narrow aperture just sufficient to carry a corpse through. The council overruled, and little George, instead of being slain, was conveyed living to the dead-house about sunset. The dead were piled on each side, leaving a narrow aisle between, and on one of these was placed the deceased boy; and, bound tightly till the purple, quivering flesh puffed above the strong bark cords, that he might die very soon, the living was placed by his side, his face to his till the very lips met, and extending along limb to limb and foot to foot, and nestled down into his couch of rottenness, to impede his breathing as far as possible and smother his cries.

Bancroft [95] states that—

The slaves sacrificed at the graves by the Aztecs and Tarascos were selected from various trades and professions, and took with them the most cherished articles of the master and the implements of their trade wherewith to supply his wants—

while among certain of the Central American tribe death was voluntary, wives, attendants, slaves, friends, and relations sacrificing themselves by means of a vegetable poison.

To the mind of a savage man unimpressed with the idea that self-murder is forbidden by law or custom, there can seem no reason why, if he so wills, he should not follow his beloved chief, master, or friend to the "happy other world;" and when this is remembered we need not feel astonished as we read of accounts in which scores of self immolations are related. It is quite likely that among our own people similar customs might be followed did not the law and society frown down such proceedings. In fact the daily prints occasionally inform us, notwithstanding the restraints mentioned, that sacrifices do take place on the occasion of the death of a beloved one.

FEASTS.

In Beltrami [96] an account is given of the funeral ceremonies of one of the tribes of the west, including a description of the feast which took place before the body was consigned to its final resting-place:

> I was a spectator of the funeral ceremony performed in honor of the manes of *Cloudy Weather's* son-in-law, whose body had remained with the Sioux, and was suspected to have furnished one of their repasts. What appeared not a little singular and indeed ludicrous in this funeral comedy was the contrast exhibited by the terrific lamentations and yells of one part of the company while the others were singing and dancing with all their might.

> At another funeral ceremony for a member of the *Grand Medicine*, and at which as *a man of another world* I was permitted to attend, the same practice occurred. But at the feast which took place on that occasion an allowance was served up for the deceased out of every article of which it consisted, while others were beating, wounding, and torturing themselves, and letting their blood flow both over the dead man and his provisions, thinking possibly that this was the most palatable seasoning for the latter which they could possibly supply. His wife furnished out an entertainment present for him of all her hair and rags, with which, together with his arms, his provisions, his ornaments, and his mystic medicine bag, he was wrapped up in the skin which had been his last covering when alive. He was then tied round with the bark of some particular trees which they use for making cords, and bonds of a very firm texture and hold (the only ones indeed which they have), and instead of being buried in the earth was hung up to a large oak. The reason of this was that, as his favorite Manitou was the eagle, his spirit would be enabled more easily from such a situation to fly with him to Paradise.

Hind [97] mentions an account of a burial feast by De Brebeuf which occurred among the Hurons of New York:

> The Jesuit missionary, P. de Brebeuf, who assisted at one of the "feasts of the dead" at the village of Ossosane, before the dispersion of the Hurons, relates that the ceremony took place in the presence of 2,000 Indians, who offered 1,300 presents at the common tomb, in testimony of their grief. The people belonging to five large villages deposited the bones of their dead in a gigantic shroud, composed of forty-eight

robes, each robe being made of ten beaver skins. After being carefully wrapped in this shroud, they were placed between moss and bark. A wall of stones was built around this vast ossuary to preserve it from profanation. Before covering the bones with earth a few grains of Indian corn were thrown by the women upon the sacred relics. According to the superstitious belief of the Hurons the souls of the dead remain near the bodies until the "feast of the dead"; after which ceremony they become free, and can at once depart for the land of spirits, which they believe to be situated in the regions of the setting sun.

Ossuaries have not been used by savage nations alone, for the custom of exhuming the bones of the dead after a certain period, and collecting them in suitable receptacles, is well known to have been practiced in Italy, Switzerland, and France. The writer saw in the church-yard of Zug, Switzerland, in 1857, a slatted pen containing the remains of hundreds of individuals. These had been dug up from the grave-yard and preserved in the manner indicated. The catacombs of Naples and Paris afford examples of burial ossuaries.

SUPERSTITION REGARDING BURIAL FEASTS.

The following account is by Dr. S. G. Wright, acting physician to the Leech Lake Agency, Minnesota:—

Pagan Indians or those who have not become Christians still adhere to the ancient practice of feasting at the grave of departed friends; the object is to feast with the departed; that is, they believe that while they partake of the visible material the departed spirit partakes at the same time of the spirit that dwells in the food. From ancient time it was customary to bury with the dead various articles, such especially as were most valued in lifetime. The idea was that there was a spirit dwelling in the article represented by the material article; thus the war-club contained a spiritual war-club, the pipe a spiritual pipe, which could be used by the departed in another world. These several spiritual implements were supposed, of course, to accompany the soul, to be used also on the way to its final abode. This habit has now ceased.

FOOD.

This subject has been sufficiently mentioned elsewhere in connection with other matters and does not need to be now repeated. It has been an almost universal custom throughout the whole extent of the country to place food in or near the grave of deceased persons.

DANCES.

Gymnastic exercises, dignified with this name, upon the occasion of a death or funeral, were common to many tribes. It is thus described by Morgan: [98]

> An occasional and very singular figure was called the "dance for the dead." It was known as the *O-hé-wä*. It was danced by the women alone. The music was entirely vocal, a select band of singers being stationed in the center of the room. To the songs for the dead which they sang the dancers joined in chorus. It was plaintive and mournful music. This dance was usually separate from all councils and the only dance of the occasion. It was commenced at dusk or soon after and continued until towards morning, when the shades of the dead who were believed to be present and participate in the dance were supposed to disappear. The dance was had whenever a family which had lost a member called for it, which was usually a year after the event. In the spring and fall it was often given for all the dead indiscriminately, who were believed then to revisit the earth and join in the dance.

The interesting account which now follows is by Stephen Powers [99] and relates to the Yo-kaí-a of California, containing other matters of importance pertaining to burial:

> I paid a visit to their camp four miles below Ukiah, and finding there a unique kind of assembly-house, desired to enter and examine it, but was not allowed to do so until I had gained the confidence of the old sexton by a few friendly words and the tender of a silver half dollar. The pit of it was about 50 feet in diameter and 4 or 5 feet deep, and it was so heavily roofed with earth that the interior was damp and somber as a tomb. It looked like a low tumulus, and was provided with a tunnel-like entrance about 10 feet long and 4 feet high, and leading down to a level with the floor of the pit. The mouth of the tunnel was closed with brush, and the venerable sexton would not remove it until he had slowly and devoutly paced several times to and fro before the entrance.

166

Passing in I found the massive roof supported by a number of peeled poles painted white and ringed with black and ornamented with rude devices. The floor was covered thick and green with sprouting wheat, which had been scattered to feed the spirit of the captain of the tribe, lately deceased. Not long afterwards a deputation of the Senèl come up to condole with the Yo-kaí-a on the loss of their chief, and a dance or series of dances was held which lasted three days. During this time of course the Senèl were the guests of the Yo-kaí-a, and the latter were subjected to a considerable expense. I was prevented by other engagements from being present, and shall be obliged to depend on the description of an eye-witness, Mr. John Tenney, whose account is here given with a few changes:

There are four officials connected with the building, who are probably chosen to preserve order and to allow no intruders. They are the assistants of the chief. The invitation to attend was from one of them, and admission was given by the same. These four wore black vests trimmed with red flannel and shell ornaments. The chief made no special display on the occasion. In addition to these four, who were officers of the assembly-chamber, there were an old man and a young woman, who seemed to be priest and priestess. The young woman was dressed differently from any other, the rest dressing in plain calico dresses. Her dress was white covered with spots of red flannel, cut in neat figure, ornamented with shells. It looked gorgeous and denoted some office, the name of which I could not ascertain. Before the visitors were ready to enter, the older men of the tribe were reclining around the fire smoking and chatting. As the ceremonies were about to commence, the old man and young woman were summoned, and, standing at the end opposite the entrance, they inaugurated the exercises by a brief service, which seemed to be a dedication of the house to the exercises about to commence. Each of them spoke a few words, joined in a brief chant, and the house was thrown open for their visitors. They staid at their post until the visitors entered and were seated on one side of the room. After the visitors then others were seated, making about 200 in all, though there was plenty of room in the center for the dancing.

Before the dance commented the chief of the visiting tribe made a brief speech in which he no doubt referred to the death of the chief of the Yo-kaí-a, and offered the sympathy of his tribe in this loss. As he spoke, some of the women scarcely refrained from crying out, and with difficulty they suppressed their sobs. I presume that he proposed a few moments of mourning, for when he stopped the whole assemblage burst forth into a bitter wailing, some screaming as if in agony. The whole thing created such a din that I was compelled to stop my ears. The air was rent and pierced with their cries. This wailing and shedding of tears lasted about three or five minutes, though it seemed to last a half hour. At a given signal they ceased, wiped their eyes, and quieted down.

Then preparations were made for the dance. One end of the room was set aside for the dressing-room. The chief actors wens five men, who were muscular and agile. They were profusely decorated with paint and feathers, while white and dark stripes covered their bodies. They were girt about the middle with cloth of bright colors, sometimes with variegated shawls. A feather mantle hung from the shoulder, reaching below the knee; strings of shells ornamented the neck, while their heads were covered with a crown of eagle feathers. They had whistles in their months as they danced, swaying their heads, bending and whirling their bodies; every muscle seemed to be exercised, and the feather ornaments quivered with light. They were agile and graceful as they bounded about in the sinuous course of the dance.

The five men were assisted by a semicircle of twenty women, who only marked time by stepping up and down with short step. They always took their places first and disappeared first, the men making their exit gracefully one by one. The dresses of the women were suitable for the occasion. They were white dresses, trimmed heavily with black velvet. The stripes were about three inches wide, some plain and others edged like saw teeth. This was an indication of their mourning for the dead chief, in whose honor they had prepared that style of dancing. Strings of haliotis and pachydesma shell beads encircled their necks, and around their waists were belts heavily loaded with the same material. Their head-dresses were more showy than those of the men. The head was encircled with a bandeau of otters' or beavers' fur, to which were attached short wires standing out in all directions, with glass or shell beads strung on them, and at the tips little feather flags and quail plumes. Surmounting all was a pyramidal plume of feathers, black, gray, and scarlet, the top generally being a bright scarlet bunch, waving and tossing very beautifully. All these combined gave their heads a very brilliant and spangled appearance.

The first day the dance was slow and funereal, in honor of the Yo-kaí-a chief who died a short time before. The music was mournful and simple, being a monotonous chant in which only two tones were used, accompanied with a rattling of split sticks and stamping on a hollow slab. The second day the dance was more lively on the part of the men, the music was better, employing airs which had a greater range of tune, and the women generally joined in the chorus. The dress of the women was not so beautiful, as they appeared in ordinary calico. The third day, if observed in accordance with Indian custom, the dancing was still more lively and the proceedings more gay, just as the coming home from a Christian funeral is apt to be much more jolly than the going out.

A Yo-kaí-a widow's style of mourning is peculiar. In addition to the usual evidences of grief, she mingles the ashes of her dead husband with pitch, making a white tar or unguent, with which she smears a band about two inches wide all around the edge of the hair (which is previously cut off close to the head), so that at a little distance she appears to be wearing a white chaplet.

It is their custom to "feed the spirits of the dead" for the space of one year by going daily to places which they were accustomed to frequent while living, where they sprinkle pinole upon the ground. A Yo-kaí-a mother who has lost her babe goes every day for a year to some place where her little one played when alive, or to the spot where the body was burned, and milks her breasts into the air. This is accompanied by plaintive mourning and weeping and piteous calling upon her little one to return, and sometimes she sings a hoarse and melancholy chant, and dances with a wild static swaying of the body.

SONGS.

It has nearly always been customary to sing songs at not only funerals, but for varying periods of time afterwards, although these chants may no doubt occasionally have been simply wailing or mournful ejaculation. A writer [100] mentions it as follows:

At almost all funerals there is an irregular crying kind of singing, with no accompaniments, but generally all do not sing the same melody at the same time in unison. Several may sing the same song and at the

169

same time, but each begins and finishes when he or she may wish. Often for weeks, or even months, after the decease of a dear friend, a living one, usually a woman, will sit by her house and sing or cry by the hour, and they also sing for a short time when they visit the grave or meet an esteemed friend whom they have not seen since the decease. At the funeral both men and women sing. No. 11 I have heard more frequently some time after the funeral, and No. 12 at the time of the funeral, by the Twanas. (For song see p. 251 of the magazine quoted.) The words are simply an exclamation of grief, as our word "alas," but they also have other words which they use, and sometimes they use merely the syllable *la*. Often the notes are sung in this order, and sometimes not, but in some order the notes *do* and *la*, and occasionally *mi*, are sung.

Some pages back will be found a reference, and the words of a peculiar death dirge sung by the Senèl of California, as related by Mr. Powers. It is as follows:

Hel-lel-li-ly,

Hel-lel-lo,

Hel-lel-lo.

Mr. John Campbell, of Montreal, Canada, has kindly called the attention of the writer to death songs very similar in character; for instance, the Basques of Spain ululate thus:

Lelo il Lelo, Lelo dead Lelo,

Lelo il Lelo,

Lelo zarat, Lelo zara,

Il Lelon killed Lelo.

This was called the "ululating Lelo." Mr. Campbell says:

This again connects with the Linus or Ailinus of the Greeks and Egyptians * * * which Wilkinson connects with the Coptic "ya lay-lee-ya lail." The Alleluia which Lescarbot heard the South Americans sing must have been the same wail. The Greek verb ὀλολύζω and the Latin ululare, with an English howl and wail, are probably derived from this ancient form of lamentation.

In our own time a writer on the manner and customs of the Creeks describes a peculiar alleluia or hallelujah he heard, from which he inferred that the American Indians must be the descendants of the lost tribes of Israel.

GAMES.

It is not proposed to describe under this heading examples of those athletic and gymnastic performances following the death of a person which have been described by Lafitau, but simply to call attention to a practice as a secondary or adjunct part of the funeral rites, which consists in gambling for the possession of the property of the defunct. Dr. Charles E. McChesney, U.S.A., who for some time was stationed among the Wahpeton and Sisseton Sioux, furnishes a detailed and interesting account of what is called the "ghost gamble." This is played with marked wild-plum stones. So far as ascertained it is peculiar to the Sioux. Figure 33 appears as a fair illustration of the manner in which this game is played.

F_{IG}. 33.—Ghost Gamble.

After the death of a wealthy Indian the near relatives take charge of the effects, and at a stated time—usually at the time of the first feast held over the bundle containing the lock of hair—they are divided into many small piles, so as to give all the Indians invited to play an opportunity to win something. One Indian is selected to represent the ghost and he plays against all the others, who are not required to stake anything on the result, but simply invited to take part in the ceremony, which is usually held in the lodge of the dead person, in which is contained the bundle inclosing the lock of hair. In cases where the ghost himself is not wealthy the stakes are furnished by his rich friends, should he have any. The players are called in one at a time, and play singly against the ghost's representative, the gambling being done in recent years by means of cards. If the invited player succeeds in beating the ghost, he takes one of the piles of goods and passes out, when another is invited to play, &c., until all the piles of goods are won. In cases of men only the men play, and in cases of women the women only take part in the ceremony.

Before white men came among these Indians and taught them many of his improved vices, this game was played by means of figured plum-seeds, the men using eight and the women seven seeds, figured as follows, and shown in Figure 34.

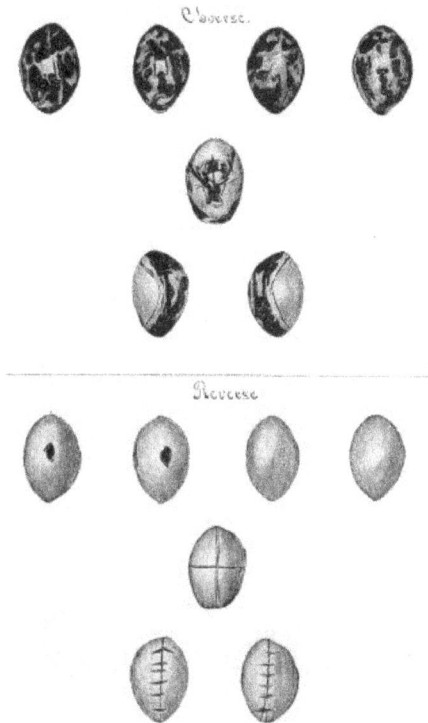

F_{IG}. 34.—Figured Plum Stones.

Two seeds are simply blackened on one side, the reverse containing nothing. Two seeds are black on one side, with a small spot of the color of the seed left in the center, the reverse side having a black spot in the center, the body being plain. Two seeds have a buffalo's head on one side and the reverse simply two crossed black lines. There is but one seed of this kind in the set used by the women. Two seeds have half of one side blackened and the rest left plain, so as to represent a half moon; the reverse has a black longitudinal line crossed at right angles by six small ones. There are six throws whereby the player can win, and five that entitle him to another throw. The winning throws are as follows, each winner taking a pile of the ghost's goods:

FIG. 35.—Winning Throw No. 1.

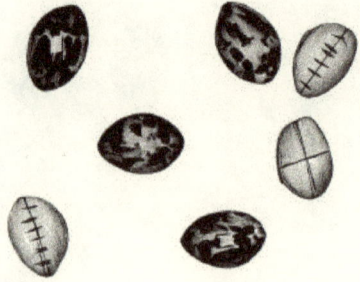

FIG. 36.—Winning Throw No. 2.

FIG. 37.—Winning Throw No. 3.

FIG. 38.—Winning Throw No. 4.

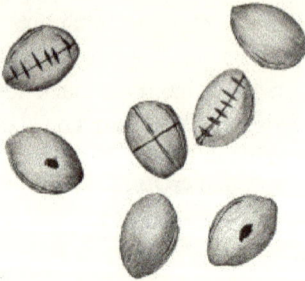

FIG. 39.—Winning Throw No. 5.

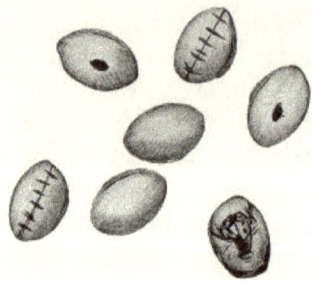

FIG. 40.—Winning Throw No. 6.

Two plain ones up, two plain with black spots up, buffalo's head up, and two half moons up wins a pile. Two plain black ones up, two black with natural spots up, two longitudinally crossed ones up, and the transversely crossed one up wins a pile. Two plain black ones up, two black with natural spots up, two half moons up, and the transversely crossed one up wins a pile. Two plain black ones, two

174

black with natural spots up, two half moons up, and the buffalo's head up wins a pile. Two plain ones up, two with black spots up, two longitudinally crossed ones up, and the transversely crossed one up wins a pile. Two plain ones up, two with black spots up, buffalo's head up, and two long crossed up wins a pile. The following auxiliary throws entitle to another chance to win: two plain ones up, two with black spots up, one half moon up, one longitudinally crossed one up, and buffalo's head up gives another throw, and on this throw, if the two plain ones up and two with black spots with either of the half moons or buffalo's head up, the player takes a pile. Two plain ones up, two with black spots up, two half moons up, and the transversely crossed one up entitles to another throw, when, if all of the black sides come up, excepting one, the throw wins. One of the plain ones up and all the rest with black sides up gives another throw, and the same then turning up wins. One of the plain black ones up with that side up of all the others having the least black on gives another throw, when the same turning up again wins. One half moon up, with that side up of all the others having the least black on gives another throw, and if the throw is then duplicated it wins. The eighth seed, used by the men, has its place in their game whenever its facings are mentioned above.

I transmit with this paper a set of these figured seeds, which can be used to illustrate the game if desired. These seeds are said to be nearly a hundred years old, and sets of them are now very rare.

Fɪɢ. 41.—Auxiliary Throw No. 1.

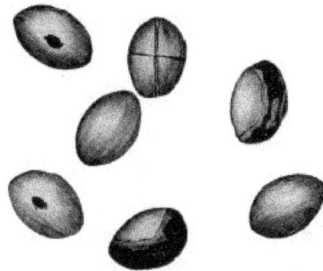

Fɪɢ. 42.—Auxiliary Throw No. 2.

F_{IG}. 43.—Auxiliary Throw No. 3.   F_{IG}. 44.—Auxiliary Throw No. 4.

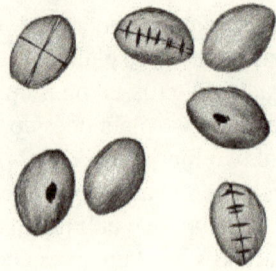

F_{IG}. 45.—Auxiliary throw No 5.

For assisting in obtaining this account Dr. McChesney acknowledges his indebtedness to Dr. C. C. Miller, physician to the Sisseton Indian Agency.

Figures 35 to 45 represent the appearance of the plum stones and the different throws; these have been carefully drawn from the set of stones sent by Dr. McChesney.

POSTS.

These are placed at the head or foot of the grave, or at both ends, and have painted or carved on them a history of the deceased or his family, certain totemic characters, or, according to Schoolcraft, not the achievements of the dead, but of those warriors who assisted and danced at the interment. The northwest tribes and others frequently plant poles near the graves, suspending therefrom bite of rag, flags, horses' tails, &c. The custom among the present Indians does not exist to any extent. Beltrami [101] speaks of it as follows:

Here I saw a most singular union. One of these graves was

176

surmounted by a cross, whilst upon another close to it a trunk of a tree was raised, covered with hieroglyphics recording the number of enemies slain by the tenant of the tomb and several of his tutelary Manitous.

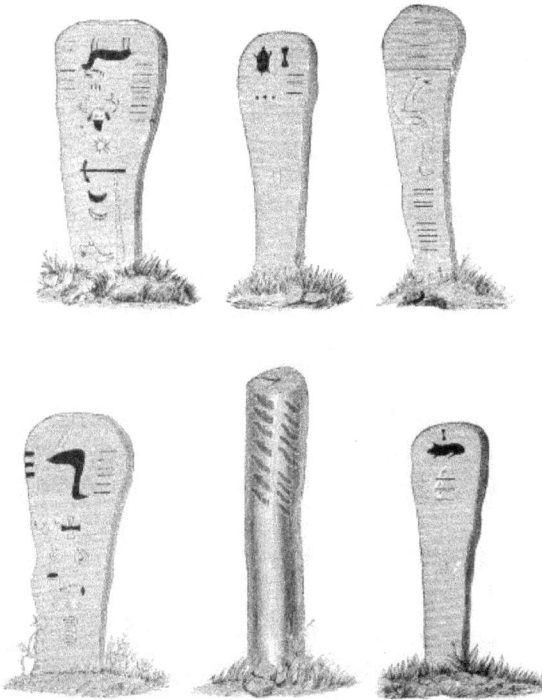

FIG. 46.—Grave Posts.

The following extract from Schoolcraft [102] relates to the burial posts used by the Sioux and Chippewas. Figure 46 is after the picture given by this author in connection with the account quoted:

Among the Sioux and Western Chippewas, after the body had been wrapped in its best clothes and ornaments, it is then placed on a scaffold or in a tree until the flesh is entirely decayed, after which the bones are buried and grave-posts fixed. At the head of the grave a tubular piece of cedar or other wood, called the *adjedatig*, is set. This grave-board contains the symbolic or representative figure, which records, if it be a warrior, his totem, that is to say the symbol of his family, or surname, and such arithmetical or other devices as seem to denote how many times the deceased has been in war parties, and how many scalps he has taken from the enemy—two facts from which his reputation is essentially to be derived. It is seldom that more is attempted in the way of inscription. Often, however, distinguished chiefs have their war flag, or, in modern days, a small ensign of American fabric, displayed on a standard at the head of their graves, which is left to fly over the deceased till it is wasted by the elements. Scalps of their enemies, feathers of the bald or black eagle, the swallow-tailed falcon, or some carnivorous bird, are also placed, in such instances, on the *adjedatig*, or suspended, with offerings of various kinds, on a separate staff. But the latter are superadditions of a religious character, and belong to the class of the Ke-ke-wa-o-win-an-tig (*ante*, No. 4). The building of a funeral fire on recent graves is also a rite which belongs to the consideration of their religious faith.

FIRES.

It is extremely difficult to determine why the custom of building fires on or near graves was originated, some authors stating that the soul thereby underwent a certain process of purification, others that demons were driven away by them, and again that they were to afford light to the wandering soul setting out for the spirit land. One writer states that—

> The Algonkins believed that the fire lighted nightly on the grave was to light the spirit on its journey. By a coincidence to be explained by the universal sacredness of the number, both Algonkins and Mexicans maintained it for four nights consecutively. The former related the tradition that one of their ancestors returned from the spirit land and informed their nation that the journey thither consumed just four days, and that collecting fuel every night added much to the toil and fatigue the soul encountered, all of which could be spared it.

So it would appear that the belief existed that the fire was also intended to assist the spirit in preparing its repast.

Stephen Powers [103] gives a tradition current among the Yurok of California as to the use of fires:

> After death they keep a fire burning certain nights in the vicinity of the grave. They hold and believe, at least the "Big Indians" do, that the spirits of the departed are compelled to cross an extremely attenuated greasy pole, which bridges over the chasm of the debatable land, and

that they require the fire to light them on their darksome journey. A righteous soul traverses the pole quicker than a wicked one, hence they regulate the number of nights for burning a light according to the character for goodness or the opposite which the deceased possessed in this world.

Dr. Emil Bessels, of the Polaris expedition, informs the writer that a somewhat similar belief obtains among the Esquimaux.

Figure 47 is a fair illustration of a grave-fire; it also shows one of the grave-posts mentioned in a previous section.

F_{IG}. 47.—Grave Fire.

SUPERSTITIONS.

An entire volume might well be written which should embrace only an account of the superstitious regarding death and burial among the Indians, so thoroughly has the matter been examined and discussed by various authors, and yet so much still remains to be commented on, but in this work, which is mainly tentative, and is hoped will be provocative of future efforts, it is deemed sufficient to give only a few accounts. The first is by Dr. W. Mathews, United States Army, [104] and relates to the Hidatsa:

> When a Hidatsa dies, his shade lingers four nights around the camp or village in which he died, and then goes to the lodge of his departed kindred in the "village of the dead." When he has arrived there he is rewarded for his valor, self-denial, and ambition on earth by receiving the same regard in the one place as in the other, for there as here the brave man is honored and the coward despised. Some say that the ghosts of those that commit suicide occupy a separate part of the village, but that their condition differs in no wise from that of the others. In the next world human shades hunt and live in the shades of buffalo and other animals that have here died. There, too there are four seasons, but they come in an inverse order to the terrestrial seasons. During the four nights that the ghost is supposed to linger near his former dwelling, those who disliked or feared the deceased, and do not wish a visit from the shade, scorch with red coals a pair of moccasins which they leave at the door of the lodge. The smell of the burning leather they claim keeps the ghost out; but the true friends of the dead man take no such precautions.

From this account it will be seen that the Hidatsa as well as the Algonkins and Mexicans believed that four days were required before the spirit could finally leave the earth. Why the smell of burning leather should be offensive to spirits it would perhaps be fruitless to speculate on.

The next account, by Keating, [105] relating to the Chippewas, shows a slight analogy regarding the slippery-pole tradition already alluded to:

> The Chippewas believe that there is in man an essence entirely distinct from the body; they call it *Ochechag*, and appear to supply to it the qualities which we refer to the soul. They believe that it quits the body it the time of death, and repairs to what they term *Chekechekchekawe*; this region is supposed to be situated to the south, and on the shores of the great ocean. Previous to arriving there they meet with a stream which they are obliged to cross upon a large snake that answers the purpose of a bridge; those who die from drowning never succeed in crossing the stream; they are thrown into it and remain there forever.

Some souls come to the edge of the stream, but are prevented from passing by the snake, which threatens to devour them; these are the souls of the persons in a lethargy or trance. Being refused a passage these souls return to their bodies and reanimate them. They believe that animals have souls, and even that inorganic substances, such as kettles, &c., have in them a similar essence.

In this land of souls all are treated according to their merits. Those who have been good men are free from pain; they have no duties to perform, their time is spent in dancing and singing, and they feed upon mushrooms, which are very abundant. The souls of bad men are haunted by the phantom of the persons or things that they have injured; thus, if a man has destroyed much property the phantoms of the wrecks of this property obstruct his passage wherever he goes; if he has been cruel to his dogs or horses they also torment him after death. The ghosts of those whom during his lifetime he wronged are there permitted to avenge their injuries. They think that when a soul has crossed the stream it cannot return to its body, yet they believe in apparitions, and entertain the opinion that the spirits of the departed will frequently revisit the abodes of their friends in order to invite them to the other world, and to forewarn them of their approaching dissolution.

Stephen Powers, in his valuable work so often quoted, gives a number of examples of superstitions regarding the dead, of which the following relates to the Karok of California:

How well and truly the Karok reverence the memory of the dead is shown by the fact that the highest crime one can commit is the *pet-chi-é-ri* the mere mention of the dead relative's name. It is a deadly insult to the survivors, and can be atoned for only by the same amount of blood-money paid for willful murder. In default of that they will have the villain's blood. * * * At the mention of his name the mouldering skeleton turns in his grave and groans. They do not like stragglers even to inspect the burial place. * * * They believe that the soul of a good Karok goes to the "happy western land" beyond the great ocean. That they have a well-grounded assurance of an immortality beyond the grave is proven, if not otherwise, by their beautiful and poetical custom of whispering a message in the ear of the dead. * * * Believe that dancing will liberate some relative's soul from bonds of death, and restore him to earth.

According to the same author, when a Kelta dies a little bird flies away with his soul to the spirit land. If he was a bad Indian a hawk will catch the little bird and eat him up, soul and feathers, but if he was good he will reach the spirit land. Mr. Powers also states that—

> The Tolowa share in the superstitious observance for the memory of the dead which is common to the Northern Californian tribes. When I asked the chief Tahhokolli to tell me the Indian words for "father" and "mother" and certain others similar, he shook his head mournfully and said, "All dead," "All dead," "No good." They are forbidden to mention the name of the dead, as it is a deadly insult to the relatives,
> * * * and that the Mat-tóal hold that the good depart to a happy region somewhere southward in the great ocean, but the soul of a bad Indian transmigrates into a grizzly bear, which they consider, of all animals, the cousin-german of sin.

The same author who has been so freely quoted states as follows regarding some of the superstitions and beliefs of the Modocs:

> * * * It has always been one of the most passionate desires among the Modok, as well as their neighbors, the Shastika, to live, die, and be buried where they were born. Some of their usages in regard to the dead and their burial may be gathered from an incident that occurred while the captives of 1873 were on their way from the Lava Beds to Fort Klamath, as it was described by an eye-witness. Curly-headed Jack, a prominent warrior, committed suicide with a pistol. His mother and female friends gathered about him and set up a dismal wailing; they besmeared themselves with his blood and endeavored by other Indian customs to restore his life. The mother took his head in her lap and scooped the blood from his ear, another old woman placed her hand upon his heart, and a third blew in his face. The sight of the group—these poor old women, whose grief was unfeigned, and the dying man—was terrible in its sadness. Outside the tent stood Bogus-Charley, Huka Jim, Shucknasty Jim, Steamboat Frank, Curly-headed Doctor, and others who had been the dying man's companions from childhood, all affected to tears. When he was lowered into the grave, before the soldiers began to cover the body, Huka Jim was seen running eagerly about the camp trying to exchange a two-dollar bill of currency for silver. He owed the dead warrior that amount of money, and he had grave doubts whether the currency would be of any use to him in the other world—sad commentary on our national currency!—and desired to have the coin instead. Procuring it from one of the

soldiers he cast it in and seemed greatly relieved. All the dead man's other effects, consisting of clothing, trinkets, and a half dollar, were interred with him, together with some root-flour as victual for the journey to the spirit land.

The superstitious fear Indians have of the dead or spirit of the dead may be observed from the following narrative by Swan. [106] It regards the natives of Washington Territory:

My opinion about the cause of these deserted villages is this: It is the universal custom with these Indians never to live in a lodge where a person has died. If a person of importance dies, the lodge is usually burned down, or taken down and removed to some other part of the bay; and it can be readily seen that in the case of the Palux Indians, who had been attacked by the Chehalis people, as before stated, their relatives chose at once to leave for some other place. This objection to living in a lodge where a person has died is the reason why their sick slaves are invariably carried out into the woods, where they remain either to recover or die. There is, however, no disputing the fact that an immense mortality has occurred among these people, and they are now reduced to a mere handful.

The great superstitious dread these Indians have for a dead person, and their horror of touching a corpse, oftentimes give rise to a difficulty as to who shall perform the funeral ceremonies; for any person who handles a dead body must not eat of salmon or sturgeon for thirty days. Sometimes, in cases of small-pox, I have known them leave the corpse in the lodge, and all remove elsewhere; and in two instances that came to my knowledge, the whites had to burn the lodges, with the bodies in them, to prevent infection.

So, in the instances I have before mentioned, where we had buried Indians, not one of their friends or relatives could be seen. All kept in their lodges, singing and drumming to keep away the spirits of the dead.

According to Bancroft [107]—

The Tlascaltecs supposed that the common people were after death transformed into beetles and disgusting objects, while the nobler became stars and beautiful birds.

The Mosquito Indians of Central America studiously and superstitiously avoid mentioning the name of the dead, in this regard resembling those of our own country.

Enough of illustrative examples have now been given, it is thought, to enable observers to thoroughly comprehend the scope of the proposed final volume on the mortuary customs of North American Indians, and while much more might have been added from the stored-up material on hand, it has not been deemed advisable at this time to yield to a desire for amplification. The reader will notice, as in the previous paper, that discussion has been avoided as foreign to the present purpose of the volume, which is intended, as has been already stated, simply to induce further investigation and contribution from careful and conscientious observers. From a perusal of the excerpts from books and correspondence given will be seen what facts are useful and needed; in short, most of them may serve as copies for preparation of similar material.

To assist observers, the queries published in the former volume are also given.

1st. NAME OF THE TRIBE; present appellation; former, if differing any; and that used by the Indians themselves.

2d. LOCALITY, PRESENT AND FORMER.—The response should give the range of the tribe and be full and geographically accurate.

3d. DEATHS AND FUNERAL CEREMONIES; what are the important and characteristic facts connected with these subjects? How is the corpse prepared after death and disposed of? How long is it retained? Is it spoken to after death as if alive? when and where? What is the character of the addresses? What articles are deposited with it; and why? Is food put in the grave, or in or near it afterwards? Is this said to be an ancient custom? Are persons of the same gens buried together; and is the clan distinction obsolete, or did it ever prevail?

4th. MANNER OF BURIAL, ANCIENT AND MODERN; STRUCTURE AND POSITION OF THE GRAVES; CREMATION.—Are burials usually made in high and dry grounds? Have mounds or tumuli been erected in modern times over the dead? How is the grave prepared and finished? What position are bodies placed in? Give reasons therefor if possible. If cremation is or was practiced, describe the process, disposal of the ashes, and origin of custom or traditions relating thereto. Are the dead ever eaten by the survivors? Are bodies deposited in springs or in any body of water? Are scaffolds or trees used as burial places; if so, describe construction of the former and how the corpse is prepared, and whether placed in skins or boxes. Are bodies placed in canoes? State whether they are suspended from trees, put on scaffolds or posts, allowed to float on the water or sunk beneath it, or buried in the ground. Can any reasons be

184

given for the prevalence of any one or all of the methods? Are burial posts or slabs used, plain, or marked, with flags or other insignia of position of deceased. Describe embalmment, mummification, desiccation, or if antiseptic precautions are taken, and subsequent disposal of remains. Are bones collected and reinterred; describe ceremonies, if any, whether modern or ancient. If charnel houses exist or have been used, describe them.

5th. MOURNING OBSERVANCES.—Is scarification practiced, or personal mutilation? What is the garb or sign of mourning? How are the dead lamented? Are periodical visits made to the grave? Do widows carry symbols of their deceased children or husbands, and for how long? Are sacrifices, human or otherwise, voluntary or involuntary, offered? Are fires kindled on graves; why, and at what time, and for how long?

6th. BURIAL TRADITIONS AND SUPERSTITIONS.—Give in full all that can be learned on these subjects, as they are full of interest and very important.

In short, every fact bearing on the disposal of the dead; and correlative customs are needed, and details should be as succinct and full as possible.

One of the most important matters upon which information is needed is the "why" and "wherefore" for every rite and custom; for, as a rule, observers are content to simply state a certain occurrence as a fact, but take very little trouble to inquire the reason for it.

Any material the result of careful observation will be most gratefully received and acknowledged in the final volume; but the writer must here confess the lasting obligation he is under to those who have already contributed, a number so large that limited space precludes a mention of their individual names.

Criticism and comments are earnestly invited from all those interested in the special subject of this paper and anthropology in general. Contributions are also requested from persons acquainted with curious forms of burial prevailing among other tribes of savage men.

The lithographs which illustrate this paper have been made by Thos. Sinclair & Son, of Philadelphia, Pa., after original drawings made by Mr. W. H. Holmes, who has with great kindness superintended their preparation.

FOOTNOTES

1. Hist. Ind. Tribes of U.S., 1853, pt. 3, p. 193.

2. Antiq. of Southern Indians, 1873, pp. 108-110.

3. Hist. of Carolina, 1714, p. 181.

4. Hist. Ind. Tribes of U.S., 1855, pt. 5, p. 270.

5. Rep. Smithsonian Institution, 1871, p. 407.

6. Voy. dans l'Arizona, in Bull. Soc. de Géographie, 1877.

7. Nat. Races Pacif. States 1874, vol. 1, p. 555.

8. Cont. to N. A. Ethnol., 1877, vol. iii, p. 133.

9. L'incertitude des Signes de la Mort, 1749, t. 1, p. 439.

10. Rites of Funeral, Ancient and Modern, 1683, p. 45.

11. Schoolcraft Hist. Ind. Tribes of the United States, 1853, Pt. 3, p. 140.

12. U.S. Geol. Surv. of Terr. 1876, p. 473.

13. Life and adventures of Moses Van Campen, 1841, p. 252.

14. Trans. Amer. Antiq. Soc., 1830, vol i, p. 302.

15. Antiquities of Tennessee. Smith. Inst. Cont. to Knowledge. No. 259, 1876. Pp. 1, 8, 37, 52, 55, 82.

16. Pop. Sc. Month., Sept., 1877, p. 577.

17. Nat. Races of the Pacific States, 1874, vol. i, p. 780.

18. A detailed account of this exploration, with many illustrations, will be found in the Eleventh Annual Report of the Peabody Museum, Cambridge, 1878.

19. Trans. Amer. Antiq. Soc., 1820, vol. i, p. 174 *et seq.*

20. American Naturalist, 1877, xi, No. 11, p. 688.

21. Proc. Am. Ass. Adv. of Science, 1875, p. 288.

22. Bartram's Travels, 1791, p. 513.

23. Bartram's Travels, 1791, p. 515.

24. A Concise Nat. Hist. of East and West Florida, 1775.

25. Mem. Hist. sur la Louisiane, 1753, vol. i, pp. 241-243.

26. Uncivilized Races of the World, 1870, vol i, p. 464.

27. Rep. Smithsonian Inst., 1867, p. 406.

28. Contrib. to N. A. Ethnol., 1877, vol. 1, p. 62.

29. Hist. of Virginia, 1722, p. 185.

30. Collection of Voyages, 1812, vol. xiii, p. 39.

31. Hist. Ind. Tribes United States, 1854, Part IV, pp. 155 *et seq.*

32. Trans. Amer. Antiq. Soc., 1820, vol. 1, p. 360.

33. Letter to Samuel M. Burnside, in Trans. and Coll. Amer. Antiq. Soc., 1820, vol. 1, p. 318.

34. A mummy of this kind, of a person of mature age, discovered in Kentucky, is now in the cabinet of the American Antiquarian Society. It is a female. Several human bodies were found enwrapped carefully in skins and cloths. They were inhumed below the floor of the cave; *inhumed*, and not lodged in catacombs.

35. Cont. to N. A. Ethnol., 1877, vol. i, p. 89.

36. Billings' Exped., 1802, p. 161.

37. Pre-historic Races, 1873, p. 199.

38. Rawlinson's Herodotus, Book i, chap. 198, *note.*

39. Amer. Naturalist, 1876, vol. x, p. 455 et seq.

40. Manners, Customs, &c., of North American Indians, 1844, vol. ii, p. 5.

41. Uncivilized Races of the World, 1870, vol. i, p. 483.

42. Hist. de l'Amérique Septentrionale, 1753, tome ii, p. 43.

43. Pioneer Life, 1872.

44. I saw the body of this woman in the tree. It was undoubtedly an exceptional case. When I came here (Rock Island) the bluffs on the peninsula between Mississippi and Rock River (three miles distant) were thickly studded with Indian grave mounds, showing conclusively that subterranean was the usual mode of burial. In making roads, streets, and digging foundations, skulls, bones,

trinkets, beads, etc., in great numbers, were exhumed, proving that many things (according to the wealth or station of survivors) were deposited in the graves. In 1836 I witnessed the burial of two chiefs in the manner stated.—P. GREGG.

45. Tract No. 50, West. Reserve and North. Ohio Hist. Soc. (1879?), p. 107.

46. Hist. of Ft. Wayne, 1868, p. 284.

47. The Last Act, 1876.

48. Cont. to N. A. Ethnol., 1877, vol. iii, p. 341.

49. Hist. Indian Tribes of the United States, 1854, part IV, p. 224.

50. Adventures on the Columbia River, 1831, vol. ii, p. 387.

51. Trans. Am. Antiq. Soc., 1820, vol. i, p. 377.

52. Hist. Indian Tribes of the United States, 1853, part iii, p. 112.

53. Contrib. to N. A. Ethnol., 1877, vol iii, p. 169.

54. Amer. Naturalist, November, 1878, p. 753.

55. Proc. Dav. Acad. Nat. Sci., 1867-'76, p. 64.

56. Pre-historic Races, 1873, p. 149.

57. Proc. Acad. Nat. Sci. Phila., Nov. 1874, p. 168.

58. Amer. Naturalist, Sept., 1878, p. 629.

59. Explorations of the Valley of the Great Salt Lake of Utah, 1852, p. 43.

60. Narrative of a Voyage to the Pacific, 1831, vol. i, p. 332.

61. Nat. Races of Pac. States, 1871, vol. i, p. 780.

62. Am. Antiq. and Discov., 1838, p. 286.

63. Nat. Races of Pac. States, 1874 vol. i, p. 69.

64. Travels in Alaska, 1869, p. 100.

65. Alaska and its Resources, 1870, pp. 19, 132, 145.

66. Life on the Plains, 1854, p. 68.

67. Tour to the Lakes, 1827, p. 305.

68. Long's Exped. to the St. Peter's River, 1824, p. 332.

69. L'incertitude des signes de la Mort, 1742, tome i, p. 475, *et seq.*

70. The writer is informed by Mr. John Henry Boner that the custom still prevails not only in Pennsylvania, but at the Moravian settlement of Salem, N.C.

71. Rep. Smithsonian Inst., 1866, p. 319.

72. Uncivilized Races of the World, 1874, v. ii, p. 774, *et seq.*

73. Hist. of Florida, 1775, p. 88.

74. Antiquities of the Southern Indians, 1873, p. 105.

75. Bartram's Travels, 1791, p. 516.

76. "Some ingenious men whom I have conversed with have given it as their opinion that all those pyramidal artificial hills, usually called Indian mounds, were raised on this occasion, and are generally sepulchers. However, I am of different opinion."

77. League of the Iroquois, 1851, p. 173.

78. Myths of the New World, 1868, p. 255.

79. Hist. N. A. Indians, 1844, i, p. 90.

80. Northwest Coast, 1857, p. 185.

81. Cont. N. A. Ethnol., 1877, i., p. 200.

82. Uncivilized Races of the World, 1870, vol. i, p. 483.

83. Exploration Great Salt Lake Valley, Utah, 1859, p. 48.

84. Hist. North American Indians, 1844, vol. ii, p. 141.

85. Mœurs des Sauvages, 1724, tome ii, p. 406.

86. Autobiography of James Beckwourth, 1856, p. 269.

87. Tour to the Lakes, 1827, p. 292.

88. Nat. Races of Pacific States, 1874, vol. i, pp. 731, 744.

89. Life Among the Choctaws, 1860, p. 294.

90. Bossu's Travels (Forster's translation), 1771, p. 38.

91. At the hour intended for the ceremony, they made the victims swallow little balls or pills of tobacco, in order to make them giddy, and as it were to take the sensation of pain from them; after that they were all strangled and put upon mats, the favorite on the right,

the other wife on the left, and the others according to their rank.

<u>92.</u> The established distinctions among these Indians were as follows: The Suns, relatives of the Great Sun, held the highest rank; next come the Nobles; after them the Honorables; and last of all the common people, who were very much despised. As the nobility was propagated by the women, this contributed much to multiply it.

<u>93.</u> The Great Sun had given orders to put out all the fires, which is only done at the death of the sovereign.

<u>94.</u> Ten Years in Oregon, 1850, p. 261.

<u>95.</u> Nat. Races of Pacif. States, 1875, vol iii, p. 513.

<u>96.</u> Pilgrimage, 1828, vol. ii, p. 443.

<u>97.</u> Canadian Red River Exploring Expedition, 1860, ii, p. 164.

<u>98.</u> League of the Iroquois, 1851, p. 287.

<u>99.</u> Cont. to North American Ethnol., 1878, iii, p. 164.

<u>100.</u> Am. Antiq., April, May, June, 1879, p. 251.

<u>101.</u> Pilgrimage, 1828, ii, p. 308.

<u>102.</u> Hist. Indian Tribes of the United States, 1851, part i, p. 356.

<u>103.</u> Cont. to N. A. Ethnol., 1877, vol. ii., p. 58.

<u>104.</u> Ethnol. and Philol. of the Hidatsa Indians. U.S. Geol. Surv. of Terr., 1877, p. 409.

<u>105.</u> Long's Exped., 1824, vol. ii, p. 158.

<u>106.</u> Northwest Coast, 1857, p. 212.

<u>107.</u> Nat. Races Pacif. States, 1875, vol. iii, p. 512.